Praise for

and Lauren Rothman

"Journalists by definition are not supposed to be respectable, but, now that most of us are also on TV, we have to be at least presentable. With wit and good writing, Lauren Rothman calmly, sensibly and authoritatively shows us (and you) how."
—Howard Fineman, Huffington Post editorial director and NBC News analyst

"As a champion in the political style arena, Lauren Rothman knows the fashion secrets of the nation's power players. Now the world is lucky enough to learn her simple tricks to dressing to be a champion in your own arena."
—Alicia Quarles, Correspondent, E News

"Lauren Rothman's *Style Bible* is a must-read for students who are creating a wardrobe for their first internship or job, and will serve as a valuable guide on using style to enhance one's brand. Rothman shares her passion for style in a way that is approachable, practical, fun, and immediately relevant to students and professionals of all ages."
—Mike Schaub, Ph.D., executive director, Cawley Career Education Center, Georgetown University

"This book is beyond a style bible; it's a success bible propelling you into your best corporate future!"
—Faith Popcorn, CEO Faith Popcorn's BrainReserve

"Savvy and inspired, *Style Bible* is a solid guide for cracking corporate dress codes."
—Janet Wozniak, former senior executive, Apple Computer

STYLE

WHAT TO WEAR TO WORK

BIBLE

Lauren A. Rothman

First published by Bibliomotion, Inc.

33 Manchester Road
Brookline, MA 02446
Tel: 617-934-2427
www.bibliomotion.com

Printed in the United States of America

Library of Congress Cataloging-in-Publication Data

Rothman, Lauren A.
    Style bible : what to wear to work : the definitive guide to dressing to impress / Lauren A. Rothman, styleeauteur.
        pages cm
    Summary: "First impressions count, whether you are an intern or a CEO; Lauren A. Rothman addresses an age-old dilemma: how to be appropriate and stylish in the workplace"—Provided by publisher.
    ISBN 978-1-937134-70-9 (paperback)—ISBN 978-1-937134-71-6 (ebook)—ISBN 978-1-937134-72-3 (enhanced ebook)
    1. Fashion.   2. Clothing and dress.   3. Women's clothing.   4. Men's clothing.
5. Work clothes.   I. Title.
    TT507.R674 2013
    746.9'2—dc23
                                                2013025702

To the best-dressed guys in my life, Jason and Judah

CONTENTS

INTRODUCTION

Shopping is a sport, and I am both coach and faithful cheerleader. I have lived, loved, and breathed clothes my entire life. All my memories include the outfit I was wearing at any given time; as a kid, I remembered the first day of every school year by what I wore!

Growing up, I loved watching my mom get dressed for work. She embodied my passion for style while also instilling in me a sense of professionalism at a very young age. Identifying and abiding by dress codes, especially growing up as a Cuban American in Miami, Florida, proved to be a life skill that I turned into a career. Whether I was headed into Publix on Le Jeune Road (which required a different dress code than the one in Kendall) for weekly grocery shopping with my family or on a college tour in New England (which called for very different dress than tours at Midwestern schools), I always shared my thoughts on what everyone should wear.

When I entered the workforce, the most exciting times for me centered around shopping for a wardrobe to match my internship or job. I bought my first suit at the BCBG store in Pentagon City Mall in 1997 when I was living in Washington, D.C., for the summer and interning on Capitol Hill. Enamored with business attire, I felt a delicate balance of femininity and power in those stylish wide-leg black pants, black skirt, and fitted suit jacket. I also invested in a camel suit and supplemented with tops from Banana Republic in Georgetown, dresses and accessories from Joyce Leslie in New York City, and scarves I found at street vendors. I re-wore and restyled my modest wardrobe that summer and absolutely loved the challenge. In fact, those staples reappeared as I dressed for my own journey from the fashion closet at *Elle* magazine to the luxury boutiques of Tel Aviv's fashion district. As my clients can attest, my style philosophy of combining high and low pieces hasn't changed much!

I am honored and privileged that so many clients have let me into their closets and into their lives. I have been dressing men and women professionally for the last ten years, and I've had the opportunity to expand the style awareness of hundreds of people and lead them into the world of fashion. Working one-on-one with individuals and presenting style seminars at Fortune 500 companies through my fashion consulting company, Styleauteur, have taught me how to encourage people to embody their commitment to being better dressed. Though we may not like it, we are all judged by our image. From peers to bosses, everyone has an opinion.

As I often discuss in my column on style and politics in the *Huffington Post*, "Fashion Whip," it is important that conversations include one of the most common modes of nonverbal communication: clothing! When you are successful, you should look successful, and this book will define a "successful look" in a customizable way. Chances are very good that I've dressed someone your shape, your size, and with a job similar to yours. Whether I am on national television discussing why it's empowering for women when First Lady Michelle Obama shows off her arms or on a radio show talking about the importance of upping your style quotient, I offer tips and anecdotes that help the everyday person with the balancing act of managing his or her appearance.

Style Bible: What to Wear to Work is a user-friendly handbook for the modern professional. Our culture has reached a state of complacency with respect to style and appearance. Current as well as future leaders are missing the opportunity to experience how good it can feel to "dress up" and how much impact exceptional style gives their communication. Style at work should be professional. What happened to being polished? This book takes a stand and helps you put your best-dressed self forward.

You may or may not want to go to work on a given day but the fact is, aside from the occasional "mental health day," most of us have to report for duty. And, if you have to get dressed, you might as well do it right. Be proud to dress to impress, and always dress for the job you want, not just the fabulous one you already have!

The *Style Bible* will help anyone who interacts in a professional environment—intern to CEO, PTA mom to boardroom diva. Your style of dress can signal income, occupation, social class, ethnic and religious affiliations, attitudes toward comfort, and level of confidence. It is possible for only one item to signify who you are according to any and all of these measures, so make sure you choose the outfit or accessory that is right for you at any given time. Clothing and style convey your message and are a big part of the overall visual cue you present to your public.

Dressing for work is less formulaic today, and there is more room for employees to express their individuality. You can become a power player and convey authority and seriousness with interesting cuff links, a statement necklace, or fun shoes that will keep your look unique. The casually dressed executive is a new figure in our society, and we need to define and better understand dress codes so they can guide us in times of uncertainty.

What does your style say about you at the office? It's possible that the perception of you is completely different from the reality of who you are, and you want to help manage your messaging. Do you look approachable and warm or young and inexperienced? Professional and uncomplicated or just frumpy? Well dressed or overly trendy?

Achieving style is a process. I won't always tell you what to do (though some clients would love that!) but I will help you listen to your own voice and meet your own goals. People want instructions. They want to look good. I make style and fashion education easy, empowering, and time saving. I raise awareness about topics easily ignored: Are you wearing the right size for your shape? Is your space effectively organized for ultimate dressing success? Have you let yourself go because it's too overwhelming to figure out what works?

As much as I love fashion, trends, and even fads, my advice to clients is based on tried-and-true combinations that work in professional environments. I have interviewed countless executives, human resource professionals, and senior management at many different companies, and I have learned their visions of successful style. That's what I teach my clients, whether they are twenty-five or sixty-five, and that is what I will convey here in my book. My lessons are not about being part of the in crowd; the principles I offer here simply make sure that you don't stand out by looking too frumpy, too old, too young, or like you just don't care.

Your style quotient is always the most challenging part of dressing well, but the most important part of your style is to be neat and appropriate. And, just by choosing this book, you are demonstrating that you are willing to learn more. In chapter 1, you will learn why style matters. Next, in chapters 2 through 5, we will review fashion basics and accessories, as well as beauty and grooming habits. Chapter 6 identifies and defines dress codes in different regions and industries. Chapters 7 through 9 are favorites for many of my clients: you will learn what constitutes a proper fit, best practices for shopping your closet, and tips on how to hit the stores. Last, we shine the spotlight on you and discuss the importance of your appearance in our hyperconnected, socially driven, virtual world.

This book follows the same organic order I use in my presentations; it can be read sequentially or consulted as a reference. The individual pieces of advice are just as valuable as the whole. Men and women have a few separate sections, but most of the general advice applies to both genders.

The most difficult hurdle to overcome when matching your shape and style in the fitting room is your own mind set. My clients often think the hard part is getting into a dress or a pair of pants. Really, the most challenging thing for them is seeing what I see: that they look incredible! I hope the anecdotes throughout the book inspire you to transformational moments; to help protect my clients' privacy, some of the stories are based on recurring experiences I've had as I built my business rather than on specific individuals. Please also note that I was not compensated for mentioning any stores or brands in *Style Bible*; these are truly retailers I believe in and have been shopping with clients for years. Dressing people for work is the riskiest area of fashion, and I've had the pleasure of watching style awareness evolve in even my most risk-averse clients. It might sound counterintuitive, but the hardest part of this process is helping people understand what works for them, and the easiest is injecting style. Let the lessons begin!

1
STYLE MATTERS

A first impression is formed in less than five seconds. Do you wear your jewelry in matched sets? Dated! Do you always choose sensible shoes that don't match your outfit? Old! Do you have a stain or a hole in your clothing and think no one will notice? Sloppy! Do you think flip-flops are okay to wear to work? Young! Entitled!

Do you think this doesn't apply to you, or that you don't need help? The amount of time you have to impress upon someone that you are right for the job passes as quickly as an eye roll. Your five seconds could happen on the way into an interview, as you casually pass someone in the hall, or when you enter a conference room for that important meeting. In business, your clothes are armor that helps communicate a message of strength.

You may even be guilty of giving a candidate "elevator eyes" yourself, quickly looking at a person from head to toe, mentally reviewing every part of her look: "I have to ask her about her shoes!"; "Her hair looks like a bird's nest!"; "I wonder if that's from the new collection that just launched at Target..." We all receive (and give) the judging look regularly, whether we realize it or not. And though you might think that women are more guilty of this particular act of assessment than men, men notice the details as well.

First impressions set the stage for future possibilities. Control your image—it is yours to define. Look in a full-length mirror when you dress and see yourself as the world sees you—is your skirt too short, or are your pants wrinkled? Catch the misstep before others do. What image do you project? Is it the one you hoped to craft for yourself? Life is not a dress rehearsal, so be appropriate and on point the first time around. A professional career is full of first impressions, and nonverbal communication makes a powerful and lasting impact. As the saying goes, dress for the job you want, not just the job you have.

Matching a wardrobe to your career is important. Don't let your clothes undermine your achievements. If you have indeed climbed the ladder of success, dress like it! Don't let your awkward, inner middle-schooler knock down your confidence. We don't need that kind of self-sabotage on our way to the top. I know many highly accomplished women who have come to me in ill-fitting clothes from twenty years ago. We all get lost at transitional points along the way; come back to the mirror and have a second look.

If you want to or need to, hire someone to help shape your image, or just dedicate time to once again finding the person in the mirror you remember. Professionals can be helpful in developing your style process: identifying the right haircut and finding a style that is both manageable and fashionable are empowering. Makeup experts can show you how to camouflage blemishes and accentuate your skin with the right colors and products, shaving off years. As you begin to invest in developing your own style, find the experts who can help. Some of the best compliments I have received are from fashion-challenged clients who expect sessions with me to be like visiting the dentist: a tedious necessity for their career health. Years later, they are hooked and are scheduling me to shop with them on their birthday instead of getting a massage. These amazing partnerships with men and women from all walks of life have informed my own path and have led me to write *Style Bible: What to Wear to Work*.

On the other end of the career spectrum, those just starting out don't have any excuse for sloppiness. Great style doesn't have to come with a high price tag. Fast-fashion chains and department stores make professional clothing easily accessible. Everyone needs to pay attention to his image. Take advantage of free style resources online and visit your favorite stores for appearances and seminars from fashion experts. Malls are among my favorite places; I could pitch a tent and never leave! At a great mall, you can shop for everything you need from head to toe (on a variety of budgets), enjoy delicious snacks (I can often be found at Nordstrom Ebars across the country), and then leave with a great manicure or blowout.

My style philosophy is simple: you deserve to care about the way you look. It's not superficial to look in the mirror and confirm that what you're wearing actually fits well and is flattering. Clothing is a powerful form of communication that everyone has access to: use it to communicate confidence, a healthy self-regard, and professionalism. I have been fortunate to help shape the image of many people, ranging from high-profile politicians to wounded soldiers returning home; college students searching for their first job to seasoned executives climbing the ladder of success; and millennial tech gurus to CEOs, and my core concept remains the same. Style matters.

Style matters as much as substance. Are you dressing passively? When you walk into work every day be aware that your ensemble didn't happen by mistake. Your clothing didn't magically appear in your closet by a genie's wish. You choose what to wear each day. You tried that outfit on in a dressing room at a store, paid for it, drove it home, hung it in your closet, and decided to wear it to work. With all those steps under your control, you are ultimately responsible for how you look at work. You were not under any other influence—at least not for every part of that scenario. Own your image the same way you own your work product.

Executive Presence

Executive presence is a key quality of leadership. True leaders exude a commanding presence built upon self-confidence and a well-put-together appearance that communicates authority as soon as they enter a room. Leaders who possess executive presence aren't necessarily the most fashion forward, but they are charismatic. Their signature styles indicate an overall attention to their appearance, with well-cared-for skin, hair, nails, and teeth, in addition to a polished look. Executive presence encompasses substance (you are a go-to expert), poise (your body language, facial expressions, and posture show you are at ease), and both public speaking and listening skills, in addition to an attractive personal style and appearance. A leader who exudes this type of presence conveys passion and energy, stands tall, makes eye contact, and communicates effectively.

Executive presence is viewed as embodying leadership potential, and the way you dress, as well as the way you carry off a look, is integral to that presence. Both are important for recognition and advancement at work. A typical frustration I hear from employees, many of whom possess a number of these executive qualities, involves getting passed over for a promotion. The most difficult issue to address in my conversations with them is appearance—some don't recognize its importance, while others find the whole thing simply too confusing. Senior managers often share with me their view that a person who looks like a hot mess will be perceived as one. Ill-fitting or stained clothing, as much as disorganized files or an office in disarray, communicates a lack of attention to detail. This is not a quality befitting a true leader or someone seeking promotion.

One of my clients, Frank, asked me to help him shop for a suit for his boss's wedding. It was a destination affair in the Caribbean, and he was confused by the "resort casual" dress code, especially given that coworkers and managers would be in attendance. He and his wife were excited to get away and take advantage of the opportunity to enjoy a much-needed vacation—Frank and Lisa had a one-year-old child at home and were ready for a rare weekend of sleeping in.

I found Frank a fabulous fitted navy linen blazer to pair with tan dress slacks (a slim fit here was key for Frank's trim physique), and a light-blue windowpane-patterned shirt, polished off with a brown belt, brown loafers, and a pocket square in a brighter blue to contrast with his dress shirt. Bam! Frank looked marvelous—so marvelous, in fact, that not only did he receive many compliments, but one managing partner at the firm joked that if Frank dressed like this more often (stylish and polished, that is, not resort casual) he would get pulled into more meetings. Frank, a self-professed brainiac, was actually a bit appalled.

Anyone in Frank's position needs to get over himself. If he is truly ready to invest in his future and to actively pursue a promotion, he can't just let his paperwork do the talking. The Franks of the world need to dress the part. They are more likely to be invited into a client or senior-management meeting at the last minute if their bosses know they will represent the firm positively. If looking polished helps get a seat at the table, then check the mirror before you leave the house. It's that simple. Should you really let yourself attend a big meeting in a wrinkled shirt, stained pants, and scuffed shoes?

"Do you have a full-length mirror that you look in before leaving the house?" I ask that question in every one of my seminars, and you would be amazed to learn that only a fraction of attendees raise their hands. Unacceptable! I am very flexible on fashion guidelines—often giving perpetrators of fashion faux pas the benefit of the doubt. But I will not bend on the issue of making an effort. I have heard every excuse in the book: "I will start caring when I lose ten pounds," "when I get a raise," or "when I don't have kids running around." But the reality is, we all get too busy to care about our appearance at work until a problem arises. If you don't look at yourself in a full-length mirror, how can you possibly see yourself the same way others do?

Frank went to work every day looking as tired as he felt. His coworkers thought, "The baby must not be sleeping through the night, poor guy," while Frank thought his rolled-up sleeves were a "tell," showing others he'd been slaving away at his desk. These vastly different interpretations show that perception doesn't always match reality. Looking like a hard-working guy was Frank's style philosophy, so he shunned a well-tailored ensemble in favor of a schlumpy, ill-fitting look à la Ron Paul in the 2012 GOP race. But Frank needs the approval of partners in his firm (who dress in custom suits), not the every-day American. To ensure his future success, he needs to address his appearance to the appropriate audience.

I have worked with more than fifty companies, assessing style complaints and walking the office floors with management to understand the infractions they regularly identify in the workplace. I decipher and update dress codes, helping companies to understand them and to implement them effectively. Management's challenge with employee dress, in almost every field, is hardly about personal taste. It's about the overall lack of understanding many employees have regarding professional image and the impact their style choices have on corporate branding. Complaints range from employees coming to the office seemingly dressed for a Saturday garage cleaning to employees who appear oblivious that their clothing is too tight, too short, or too sheer for the workplace. An inappropriate clothing selection may not earn you a public reprimand, but it will definitely hinder your climb up the corporate ladder. In order to be taken seriously, set higher expectations for yourself.

Dress codes hold us accountable. They help us understand company culture and they provide proper style boundaries. If you work in creative fields such as public relations, fashion, or new media, those boundaries may be more flexible, allowing you to dabble in more daring fashion trends—your outer appearance is a reflection of the inner you. If, on the other hand, you work in a more traditional office setting like banking, consulting, accounting, or even government, it is your level of polish that will help set you apart. If your style is stifled in a conservative setting, try directing your love of edginess toward accessories.

Private schools, the military, and even retail establishments often ask their students and employees to adhere to a uniform dress code, creating a living brand ambassador both within the company and externally. My first job taught me to harness the power of a professional image. I worked for Faith Popcorn's BrainReserve, a futurist marketing consultancy in New York City, where black (skirt or pant) suits and matching pins (they resembled a planet—you could choose your color) were the standard anytime we hit the road to work with clients or even in-house when we entertained. While this uniform may have been viewed as an infringement on our style freedom, Faith had a vision: five people moving toward you in black power suits with matching lapel pins exuded a gravitas that encouraged clients to cut a check for some very unique trend-forecasting services. When a company creates a dress code, it reveals much about its culture. More than just a policy, the code is both a reflection of and an inspiration for the people who work there. A well-written dress code can improve morale and stimulate corporate pride.

In the end, Frank realized the disadvantage of always looking like a slob at the office. Though talented and driven, he had been passed over for promotion more than once. He still may not care about fashion, per se, but he has learned that his image does matter. A little fashion therapy went a long way with Frank. He now understands he can't afford to allow others to believe that he doesn't care or that he's not happy to be there. He loves his job. He may not have enlisted an expert to help him dress for everyday life, but he recognized a shopping paralysis when dressing for his boss's wedding. Together, we created a signature style that was accessible given his time and his budget, a style that coworkers would come to respect and even admire: dark suits, tailored, slim-fit, iron-free dress shirts (best shortcut ever), and polished shoes. Nothing fancy. But it helped get him a promotion in less than a year.

Fashion Is a Foreign Language

Fashion is its own language. As with any language, it has colloquialisms that you need to learn. (The last thing you want when practicing a language is to ask for a Diet Coke and be directed to the bathroom.) Your clothing is speaking, whether you like it or not, sending messages to your colleagues about where you came from (college or competing law firm) and where you want to go (corner office or mailroom). Whatever your message, it's vitally important that you avoid confusion.

This book will help you become fluent in fashion. It is a language I have been speaking since I said my very first word, *agua*, outside Neiman Marcus at Bal Harbor in Miami, Florida. I have always chased trends, played with style, and helped people identify ways to make these concepts relevant to their lifestyle. Many senior-level executives and high-profile clients I work with don't love fashion or clothing, but they do like what a positive image can deliver—confidence and leadership opportunities that lead to constituent votes, book sales, promotions, a bigger fan base, an anchor desk, and even success in their personal lives.

I certainly wouldn't want one of my clients dressing only to impress another person, because her look may come off as inauthentic. In Hollywood, it's normal to wear six-inch stilettos so the paparazzi get their shots as A-listers walk from the car to a club. In real life, our shoes have to keep on walking, and while I abhor the word "sensible" when applied to shoes, I certainly endorse combining style with comfort. They can coexist.

In order to manage your professional image and style, you should create a personal brand message. You are, after all, a walking billboard (good posture helps!) for your brand, and your nonverbal communication helps highlight the best you have to offer. Ultimately, your crafted message should read as modern and professional. Stay away from distracting messages: too young, too old, too sexy, sloppy, or tired. Maintain a hair- and skin-care routine that does not detract from your image and a wardrobe that signals an understated power. The most challenging part of this process is identifying your personal style and making it relevant and appropriate in the workplace. The styles you like and those that work for you are not always one and the same. For example, you might love cowboy boots with a suit, but that doesn't mean you should be wearing them, unless it helps you win votes with constituents. While there are a few jobs for which a highlighted, signature style like this will create positive buzz, for the majority of jobs it will simply distract from your message. Wearing a bolo tie on an interview is not appropriate in most corporate settings—even if it's *so* you. Maintaining a unique flair is appropriate, but keep it minimal—brightly colored socks, a pocket square, or, for women, a single piece of memorable jewelry.

Often we dress without ever looking in the mirror, just imagining that we will be perceived a certain way. For example, you may think, "This jacket is red, a real power piece." Or, if you are walking into a business-formal situation, you might imagine that because you're wearing a suit it automatically affords you equal status. However, if your ensemble is ill-fitting or appears awkward, it will not work for you. Our own perception of how we look does not always match what others see.

Remember what it was like to dress for your first anything—first day of school, first formal, first college interview? Recall the butterflies, and the special care you took to dot your Is and cross your Ts? It's important to continue to take that same care daily. An exercise I often run with groups at my style seminars is the twenty-four-hour hidden fashion cam. While many wear their best outfits on the days that I come to visit, sometimes I am able to catch people by surprise. The exercise runs like this: imagine a live video feed in your office capturing you all day, every day. Would you be happy with what your clothing and body language say about you? These are things I have seen in offices when people think no one is looking (or when they just don't care whether someone is): thong underwear that sticks out from pants; muffin tops; sweaters removed, and lacy, see-through camisoles worn alone; excessive cleavage; and people crossing and uncrossing their legs in chairs without proper coverage underneath. Once pointed out, these offenses are pretty easy to avoid—if you take the time at home to dress properly. Learning the language of fashion is easy when you take it in steps. Your first step is learning to maintain an appropriate image for your body type and dress code, and the second is to infuse it with style.

Parting Thoughts

Companies care about their images and, as an employee, your style choices reflect on them for better or worse. You have a responsibility to interpret a dress code appropriately.

Get in the driver's seat and manage your look. If I could write expiration dates on labels of clothing and makeup, my clients would be so much happier. It's easier to tell when the arugula has gone bad than your tube of mascara…create a routine that keeps you looking perfectly professional.

WOMEN: TEN FASHION MISTAKES TO AVOID AT THE OFFICE

1. Don't show spaghetti straps, bra straps, or excessive cleavage.
2. Camouflage VPL (visible panty lines).
3. Avoid flashing a skin belt or muffin top.
4. Don't wear sheer, tight, short, backless, strapless, or otherwise revealing clothing.
5. Don't wear stained, ripped, or frayed clothes.
6. Avoid wrinkled or ill-fitting clothes.
7. Don't wear casual leggings or yoga pants.
8. Don't wear flip-flops, Uggs, Crocs, or cowboy boots.
9. Avoid chipped or dirty nails, unshaved legs, and body odor.
10. Avoid heavy makeup and frizzy or unkempt hair.

MEN: TEN FASHION MISTAKES TO AVOID AT THE OFFICE

1. Don't wear stained, ripped, or frayed clothes.
2. Avoid wrinkled or ill-fitting clothes.
3. Steer clear of novelty ties or accessories and avoid logos.
4. Don't wear flip-flops, mandals, or Crocs.
5. Polish your shoes.
6. Condition and prevent dry or chapped skin.
7. Avoid dandruff or unruly hair.
8. Beware of weird facial hair.
9. Take proper measures to avoid body odor.
10. Don't risk overexposure: cover tattoos and unusual piercings.

2
FASHION 101 FOR WOMEN

My favorite place to people watch is inside a corporate environment. I watch men and women walk down what I call the "office runway." They walk to the communal kitchen or office supply closet, chat with friends at cubicles or in the hallways, head into conference rooms for meetings, or visit the boss in the corner office. I've walked through many companies and observed a gap in our collective education concerning what is appropriate to wear to work. We know there are rules and expectations, and we know some of them. But we're not sure how they apply to us. Our closets hold the armor we don to face the world, whether for a big meeting or lunch with the clique. Sometimes, both events evoke our insecurities.

Women in their twenties have time to shop but typically have less disposable income. Women in their thirties are in the throes of creating balance in their lives, and shopping can often tip the scale. Many women don't come up for air or seek style advice until they reach their forties. Women in their fifties and sixties often have an established uniform, and it is only when a major shift in body type occurs or a fashion trend sweeps the country that they come running for answers. There are no formal fashion classes for those twenty-two to sixty-nine, the age range of most, but not all, working women. It is important to discuss mastering the fundamentals of dress. After all, the last time some of us learned even a single rule of fashion was at our first bra fitting.

Most fashion advisors deal in guidelines rather than hard-and-fast rules, but women should understand the basics to become successful. When dressing, especially to impress, a woman needs to be able to judge when to stand out and when to minimize risk. She needs to know the right fit for her body type, as well as the role trends play in the workplace. Many women find themselves following the same rules at forty-five that they learned at twenty-three. They need a refresher course. It is critical to strike a balance between classic pieces you have in your wardrobe and the latest, hot-off-the-runway trends.

Let's review some style basics about the clothing that's hanging in your closet as well as those pieces you can easily purchase to update your wardrobe and help you dress to impress:

- The third piece
- Suiting
- Pants
- Skirts
- Tops
- Dresses
- Coats

The Third Piece

I never leave home without a "third piece." It could be a sleek, cobalt blue, silk blazer worn with dark trouser jeans on a casual Friday, a crème cable-knit sweater coat paired with ivory cashmere slacks for a cozy Tuesday, or a black ruffle shawl over a belted little black dress (LBD) to move from day to night. The third piece is my "it" piece. My signature.

The magic of a third piece is that, instead of defaulting to a suit-like blazer, your jacket can be unstructured or tailored; swingy; cropped, or long; peplum-style; collarless; double-breasted or single-breasted; or textured. Obviously, this is one of my favorite components of any outfit, and I've hardly ever let a woman leave my fitting room without wearing a signature third piece. For me, a look is simply not complete without it. A jacket, blazer, sweater, cardigan, or sometimes even a great belt or statement piece of jewelry can serve as a third piece. The third piece is one that "makes" your outfit. In a professional environment, this is most often your jacket.

The Jacket

The jacket communicates power. It says *listen* and *look at me*. Non-verbal cues are vitally important. If you can send a power message across the conference room by simply wearing a jacket, do it. The jacket says, "I took an extra step this morning." If your dress code isn't strictly business-formal attire, wearing a jacket can indicate you are dressing to impress and dressing for the job you want. Don't dress "old"—dress "up."

The jacket can be a traditional blazer style (perhaps with a fun lining, which you can reveal by rolling up the cuff for a more casual look) or one with a modern shawl collar and tie belt. The possibilities range in color from light to dark, and from tried-and-true fabrics like wool and cotton to more interesting ones such as leather, tweed, or linen. Your options include interesting collars, shoulders, and sleeves, as well as buttons, zippers, and other embellishments. Try wearing a fabulous outfit that gets you mistaken for senior management at your next meeting.

Dina was a forty-three-year-old attorney who was lucky enough to look twenty-eight but, unfortunately, more often than not was mistaken for an administrative assistant or paralegal instead of partner. She was a busy working mom who barely had time for (let alone interest in) makeup and cute clothes. She had four kids at home, was happy she had stayed close to her pre-baby weight, and was confident in her skills at work. The fact that she was a partner had instilled in her a sense that she'd "made it." Dina wore schlumpy cardigans to work, paired with stretched-out yoga pants and Merrill hiking shoes. Yup, I said lawyer. Private firm.

Ladies, please don't stop trying! It hurts your credibility with a professional audience. Set an example for the next generation of women climbing the corporate ladder and impress the senior leaders who are hoping to promote you. Dina didn't really notice her behavior until she was asked to serve coffee at a meeting also attended by summer associates. They were dressed more appropriately than Dina was.

Dressing well is not about having a big budget—the principles of style are the same from intern to CEO. People will treat you in the manner you encourage them to. Dress in a way that makes your success clear to others, and no one will ask you to serve coffee again (unless you're hosting a party, and even then you might decide to hire someone else to do it).

One of Dina's associates slipped her my card, and she soon decided to give me a call, I think because she had felt embarrassed and disrespected by the coffee-serving incident. Her mental transformation was instant—there is nothing like being mistaken for the help when you are part of leadership. Whereas some need to be coached and coaxed, Dina just asked for the costume she needed to play the part she had earned long ago.

Armed with a closet full of stylish, age- and office-appropriate clothes, Dina hit the ground running with a new confidence that I think surprised even her. Stylish shoes by foot surgeon Taryn Rose were as comfy as her Merrills. Slim black pants showed off her shape but were unremarkable enough to be worn twice or more per week, and a simple black shell kept her look chic and monochromatic. The pièce de rèsistance was a bold, belted jacket that added just the right amount of subtle power. We created a wardrobe and uniform that was easy for this busy working mom to follow and replicate day after day.

The Cardigan

Sometimes simply known as a sweater, the cardigan used to hang in Grandma's closet. It has certainly come a long way. In the 1990s, sweater sets (or twin sets) rose in popularity and were paired with khakis and printed skirts on casual Fridays. In fact, people were so excited by the prospect of avoiding a suit that the sweater set became the Friday alternative. It helped that they can be worn year round and work so well in offices with temperature challenges.

The sweater set got a makeover and the open "cardi" was created— a more unstructured cardigan. This piece is sometimes longer than the typical hip length, doesn't always have buttons, and can easily be belted. It represents a fabulous new addition to the professional wardrobe that works on every body type and any age. Adding to its versatility, it can be dressed up or down. A ruffled, open, cardi sweater will easily dress up slacks; an asymmetrical style in a thinner knit is great for a more casual office.

A classic cardigan will always be in style and is often the perfect addition to a dress. However, try not to be too "matchy" to avoid either a dated or a too-young look. The sweater set is a universal go-to piece for interns and young college grads as well as administrative staff and older workers in the office.

The Duster

The longer sister of the open cardi, this is a fashion-forward favorite for a relaxed casual look that falls anywhere from mid-thigh to the knee. You will see it in blends of cashmere and wool in the winter and in lighter knits throughout the summer. Pair it with a belted sheath dress or slim-cut pants and heels. *Topper* and *sweater coat*, other well-known terms for the duster, can also refer to a more structured and slightly shorter third piece. Style them in the same manner for a modern silhouette.

The Vest

Vests have come in and out of fashion over the years. A menswear-inspired black vest is classic. Look for a fitted version that is minimally embellished to wear open over a long-sleeve, black top or patterned blouse, with chic jeans or slacks in a casual or business-casual environment. Add a statement necklace for a dash of bohemian flair.

Sweaters

The crewneck or V-neck sweater is most often seen at the office over a collared blouse or long-sleeve top. This is technically more of a layering item than a "third piece," but some women enjoy wearing this look. The biggest challenge here is showing off your shape. Some of you reading this are saying, "That's exactly why I wear sweaters!" but just because you don't intend to show off your figure doesn't mean we don't see it. A one-piece, closed sweater can add the illusion of more weight in the mid-section and arms, making you appear bigger. Think of the crewneck as the older sister of the sweatshirt. Do you really want people to see you in that at work?

Style Alert: *The three-quarter-length sleeve works well for any third piece. It will make you appear slimmer by hitting close to the waist and drawing the eye up instead of down to your hips. Also, this is a great solution for both petites and talls, who have trouble finding correct sleeve lengths off the rack.*

Suiting

Modern women's suiting is most often purchased as separates. While for many years traditional suits were sold only as sets (and some still are), many designers have finally wised up to the fact that women are not always the same size on the top and bottom. If you work in or plan to interview in a business-formal or even business-casual environment, you should have at least one well-tailored suit in your closet. For women, unlike men, the most versatile suit color to invest in is black. You can wear it to an interview—conservatively dressing it up or adding flash to dress it down. Later, either continue to treat it as a suit in a formal environment or break apart the pieces to use as the workhorses of your wardrobe.

Style Alert: *For the most expensive look (yet one that is often affordable), stick to a tropical-weight wool that works for all seasons. Stay away from polyesters and triacetates—they look cheap. Fabrics with stretch fibers help garments stay less wrinkled throughout the day.*

Pantsuit

If you are only buying one pantsuit, err on the side of classic and choose a trouser leg. This style is flattering on almost every body type and will stand the test of time. A two- or three-button jacket with a peak or notch lapel will most likely accompany this suit. Choose from a neutral-color palette for your subsequent suits after you've bought black: charcoal, medium gray, brown, and navy are all safe and stylish choices.

If you have a closet full of suits and are looking to add more excitement, change up the pant (slim, ankle, wide) or jacket styles (shawl collar, collarless, belted), or indulge in interesting dark colors like burgundy, plum, eggplant, or hunter green.

Skirt Suit

The skirt suit is a timeless and elegant classic. Women have been wearing skirts to the office much longer than they've been wearing pants. You may have many skirt suits hanging in your closet or just the one you purchased as a spare for your pantsuit. To stay current, look for a knee-length pencil skirt and a jacket. Continue to select colors from a neutral palette in seasonally appropriate fabrics. If you care to add a little flair, look for a tweed or jacquard.

Dress Suit

The dress suit is a very elegant style that works well from day to night or for dressy work situations (cocktail, networking, or client event). The jacket can be hip length, or end at the knee and accompany a sheath dress. The dress and jacket are usually in the same color (and can be sold as a set). The dress suit, with accompanying longer jacket, is a hard-to-find style, but it's a personal favorite for high-profile clients.

Pants

Pants are a staple of many women's closets. They are comfortable, versatile, and they require little maintenance. They're available in a variety of fits, fabrics, and colors. Hem them to various lengths to work with the right shoes, and select the pant leg that best enhances your figure.

Style Alert: *Remove dated styles from your closet: pleats, overly high waists, and pegged, tapered legs. Although some of these features come in and out of style, if you are harboring pants more than ten years old, they probably qualify as dated and look old.*

Here are the most popular styles for work:

Trouser Leg

The trouser leg is the most classic, flattering, and versatile of pant styles. It skims the thigh, comes in at the knee, and flares out slightly at the calf. It works on a majority of body types and will always make you look thinner. It may feature cuffs or a pressed crease down the middle for added structure and design. The ankle circumference will be a close match to the hip.

Wide Leg

A wide-leg pant is a statement maker. A dramatic style, it falls gracefully from the hip to the ankle. It can be glamorous for tall women and a staple for plus-size ones. It balances out pear and curvy body types, distracting from a larger hip area. Palazzo pants come in and out of style in this category and can add flair to a wardrobe of basics. Petites should avoid an overly wide leg or risk looking shorter.

Style Alert: *The most universally flattering fit is one where the ankle diameter is equal or close to the hip one. Lay out a pair of pants on the bed to see if this measurement matches what's hanging in your closet. Bend and bring the ankle up to the thigh area. If the widths are similar, you are creating a well-balanced look. If the thigh is larger, you will be attracting attention to that area. Shop carefully.*

Skinny Leg

The skinny pant is slim and cut close to the leg. A cousin to the skinny jean, it is hard to pull off at the office when you have a set of hips. My favorite (and more body-type versatile) version of this style in work pants hits at the ankle or slightly above: cigarette pants. Often noted as Audrey Hepburn's preferred pant style, these are fitted through the hip and thigh with a slim leg. Pair with ballet flats, knee-high boots, or heels for a super-chic retro-modern look.

Straight Leg

A straight-leg pant falls straight from hip to thigh, and knee to ankle. They are limited to straighter body types and do not flatter women who carry their weight in the hip area. A cropped, straight pant is a more versatile fit because a flash of leg helps to break up the look, and the bottom of the pant is not as narrow. This is a stylish option for a variety of body types in the warmer months.

Style Alert: *To increase the glam factor, add a colored pant to your repertoire. Red is quickly becoming a popular work-wear indulgence.*

Skirts

The basic skirt for work is knee-length. To identify the spot on your leg where a hem should end, examine your knee area in a full-length mirror. For some, this will be above the knee, while for others, it will be lower. See where the thigh starts to indent and lead into the knee? That's your starting point. Now look at the bottom part of your knee. See where it starts to curve outwards toward your calf? You want your skirt to end anywhere in that two-inch vicinity, depending on your body type, height, and proportions.

Here are the most popular styles for work:

Pencil

All skirts have their fashion "in" moments, and if you want to include only one in your work wardrobe, invest in this timeless shape. The pencil skirt (straight on top, it curves in toward the knee like the tip of a pencil) shows off your curves, though you may want a vent or kick pleat in the back for ease of movement. Select a versatile structured fabric like tropical-weight wool or heavy cotton. Pair with third pieces for an elegant business-formal look.

Some consider a straight skirt (which often accompanies suits) a pencil shape, but the key difference is that it doesn't hug the lower thigh. A straight skirt creates more of a rectangular shape—a conservative, dated silhouette.

A-Line

The flare on an A-line skirt follows the lines of a capital letter A. This look is often worn to conceal figure flaws. But remember: sometimes, the more you conceal, the more you reveal. The A-line skirt flatters straighter body types and makes women who carry more weight on the bottom appear heavier. This tailored look is appealing to a younger generation and works best in business-casual environments.

Full

Full skirts are fun and feminine. They are voluminous and can be pleated, gathered, or even full-circle skirts. They are more casual than pencil skirts but can still be sophisticated. Keep them knee length, and pair with a camisole and cardigan or a fitted, short, elbow-length blouse.

Tops

If you're dressing for the corner office, shop your closet for a third piece before selecting a top. If you wear a power third piece, don't overwhelm it with a blousy printed top; if you wear suits daily, don't just wear a shell the same color as your pinstripes "to bring out the color." Instead, when wearing a statement third piece, coordinate your top to match your pants or skirt to minimize its presence and maximize the impact of your power jacket. When matching a suit, try pulling out the main color instead of highlighting the accents.

Style Alert: *When you match your shell to your skirt or pants instead of to your jacket, you elongate your torso and give the illusion of looking slimmer. When you match it to your jacket, you look wider on top.*

When I walked into Mary's closet, I was struck by how many beautiful tops she owned. Displayed prominently and organized perfectly, they were very inviting. Mary loved color, and buying tops was her weakness. She worked in a business-formal environment and considered suits to be boring. Mary's complaint was not an uncommon one, and colorful tops made her happy. Once I inventoried Mary's collection, we saw that she had invested more than $3,000 in a relatively short time on tops.

Unfortunately, many of her suits were cheap looking and ill-fitting. Mary worked in financial services, a business-formal environment, and wore suits daily. All of them covered up her beautiful investments. Essentially, her tops were like lingerie…no one got to appreciate them but Mary.

Shop for the dress code your office environment dictates. Business formal requires a third piece. Mary could have had tremendous fun and shown off her style, investing in high-quality, high-impact pieces. Include stylish, classic, wear-alone tops in your wardrobe: wrap styles, bow-tie blouses, a classic white blouse, cowl-necks, turtlenecks, or kimono-sleeve or other interesting-sleeved tops. Of course, every season brings new trends, like the peplum top, and every winter will obviously include an array of sweaters. Leave tops for last and don't spend a lot unless they're highly visible or you're wearing them daily.

Shell versus Cami

You should stock shells and camisoles to coordinate with pants, skirts, and suits. A shell can be sleeveless (though it must be wide enough in the shoulders to cover your bra strap), cap-sleeve, short-sleeve, three-quarter-sleeve, or long-sleeve. Typically, shells are fitted, but not as tight as spaghetti-strapped camisoles. My favorite camis for work are made in a cotton-spandex blend that resists fading. "Tamis" are a new addition, combining the style of a tank with the fit of a cami. Whichever style works best for your shape, try to focus on fabrics that look fancy enough for the office instead of the gym. Buy seamless styles, and avoid showing a lacy cami at the office—this look had a trend moment but has since expired. Keep an eye on your internal thermometer—don't wear a sleeveless shell or cami if you work in a business-formal environment and plan to take off your third piece.

Dresses

Dresses play runner-up to pants in popularity at the office. But many women consider them easy to shop for and easier to wear: one item and you're done. Dresses are truly versatile: style them for cocktails or tailor them for the boardroom.

Here are the most popular styles for work:

The Sheath

The sheath dress is a classic office staple. A sleeveless version can be layered under suit jackets or third pieces of almost any style; one with sleeves can stand alone for a modern professional look. Belt the waist (where your sides curve in, or where you wish to give the illusion that they do), add a necklace and heels, and voilà—you're done. Start with a black sheath and continue to build your collection.

A shift dress is similar to a sheath but not as fitted through the waist and hips; it's not quite as dressy and works best on straighter body types. With either dress, be careful of empire waistlines; they can unflatteringly elongate the torso and make you appear heavier on the bottom.

The Wrap

Diane von Furstenberg made this style iconic. The trick to wearing wrap dresses is to tie them high and tight around your waist. This helps ensure they don't unravel and expose the bust area. I have clients who write down detailed directions or take a short video of the process in the fitting room to ensure they can replicate it at home.

Style Alert: *If you are busty, try adding a bandeau (instead of a cami) in the color of a wrap dress to help camouflage cleavage. Miss Oops makes a comfortable "Boob Tube."*

The Shirt Dress

Imagine your favorite button-front shirt…becoming a dress! It can have a fitted or full skirt, be monochromatic or printed, or feature color blocking (one color on top and another on the bottom). A slim fit on the bottom works best for straighter body types; a fuller skirt works for everyone else. If it gapes in the chest, add a bandeau for coverage or avoid this style. This dress blends in well at a business-casual office.

Coats

Outerwear can be as important as what is worn underneath. Depending on the climate in your locale, this may be the first thing people see you wearing every day. Don't leave the lasting impression of a baggy, dated overcoat or a casual, sporty raincoat. If you walk to work or use public transportation, invest in a weather-appropriate and stylish coat. If you move from car to garage and barely have use for outerwear, you may still need to invest in at least one versatile topper for professional travel.

Trench Coat

This is a must-have for executives. It travels through both time and weather effortlessly, is versatile enough to be worn two to three seasons, and is available in a variety of fabrics and colors. Opt for black with sophisticated detailing (like sheen or patent trim) if you plan to dress it up, or go with classic khaki to fulfill your inner prepster. I also like versions in metallic tones, prints, and midnight navy—double breasted and single, full-skirted and straight.

Style Alert: *Tie your trench instead of buckling the belt for a modern twist that highlights your waist.*

Winter Coat

Unless you live where it's incredibly cold and you are outside all the time, a three-quarter-length coat (to the knees) is always your best bet, and it's universally flattering. Look for a modern coat that offers style and/or helps show off your figure in wool, cashmere, or another warm material—even a thin down coat will work! A stand-up or shawl collar can be dramatic and a tie waist will help you look slimmer. When wearing a sweater or third piece, make sure it fits comfortably underneath. A wool or cashmere overcoat is traditional and, with the right fit, will always work. Coats give us a chance to showcase a bit of glamor. Choose a color and style that match your leadership aspirations. Black is assertive, grey is calming, camel is classic, and red shows flair—all are popular choices!

Wraps and Capes

Wraps and capes add drama. Both can be trimmed in fur and tossed over a third piece or top; both work well during transitional seasons. A wrap adds instant glamour. Choose a style versatile enough to be worn inside and out, or opt for a heavier one for outside use only. Capes are not just for superheroes anymore. They ease in and out of style through the years, so don't toss yours. Pair either of these fashionable pieces of outerwear with elbow-length gloves to stay warm, then walk the streets in style.

Parting Thoughts

Don't suppress your instinct to check out the way other women dress. Look at the style leaders in your community and see if their image is a tool that helps them climb the ladder of success. Are they dressing for their body type and age? Do they know how to accentuate (and camouflage) the appropriate places? Building a stylish professional wardrobe is less about how much you have and more about having the right stuff!

WORKPLACE DOS AND DON'TS

Attire

Do inspect your clothes for evidence of wear and tear: underarm stains; torn clothes, tights, or pantyhose; and worn tips and soles on shoes are not professional.

Don't look sloppy and careless in wrinkled or tight clothing. Invest in a steamer or frequent the local dry cleaner to avoid a rumpled, tired appearance. Ensure that undergarments are never visible and hemlines are the proper length.

Trends

Do keep your look sophisticated and stylish. Invest in wardrobe staples and don't indulge in too many trends at once.

(Continued)

Don't display wardrobe distractions like exposed bra straps, backless shirts, and miniskirts. When in doubt, keep your jacket or cardigan on in the office. The office runway should not be confused with a fashion show.

Accessories

Do accessorize confidently. Pearls, simple studs, and understated jewelry will let your work do the talking. Limit statement jewelry to one piece per outfit.

Don't wear flashy, noisy, oversized jewelry—set those aside for happy hour, not the office.

Footwear

Do wear bare legs—they are perfectly acceptable (if in accordance with your dress code) when you're sporting a knee-length hem and a well-moisturized leg.

Don't wear flip-flops in the summer, clunky boots in the winter, or change shoes at your desk—people will notice.

Grooming

Do look fresh and crisp: wear a touch of makeup, add hair product if necessary, and finish with lip stick or gloss for a flawless look. Remember, though, at the office less is more.

Don't make grooming mistakes: pay attention to chipped nail polish and chapped lips. Both are easily remedied.

3

FASHION 101 FOR MEN

Men are usually replenishment shoppers. You don't often find them seeking new styles—they just want more of what they already have. They see a hole, a stain, or a worn collar and, bam, off they run to the store or the Internet to replace their favorite items. Ladies, we could take a cue from this style of shopping.

The biggest challenge for men? Taking a minute to look in the mirror and see whether what they have on actually fits. I was recently in a client's closet, and on the floor were boxes and bags full of newly purchased Jos. A. Banks shirts, pants, and suits. And when I say "newly purchased," I mean purchased within the last six months. My client had stopped by his favorite store on a sale day to take advantage of the low prices and shopped to his heart's delight. However, it turns out my bargain-seeking shopper had not looked in the mirror in a very long time, because nothing he bought (or owned) really fit. And, by buying so much stuff on sale that didn't fit, he had actually spent more money than his wife, whose case he sometimes got on for buying full-price items (though her items *always* fit, and she did buy less than he).

When it comes to fashion, most women think the men in their lives have it pretty easy. And yet, while men have fewer pieces to coordinate and easier maintenance directions on their labels, some still manage to walk into work looking like slobs. The most common complaint I hear is about men in wrinkled or stained clothing. If the obvious pen mark you got on your shirt last month has remained intact after a visit to the dry cleaner, it's time to let it (or your cleaner) go. If you often stain your ties with food, keep a few spares in your desk drawer. One of the quickest ways to lose respect in the boardroom is to look messy or neglectful of your hygiene and appearance. There is an expectation that a smart presenter also be a neat dresser.

Men's style is mostly about fit. Of course, there are a few rules: match your socks to your pants instead of to your shoes. Update your belt if you move notches or the leather begins to come apart. (If you are losing weight reward yourself, and if you've just gained a few pounds, camouflage it.) Polish your shoes. Make sure your clothes are wrinkle-free. Never wear more than two rings, and consider your watch an investment piece.

Style Alert: *Matching your socks to your pants, rather than your shoes, will elongate your legs for a fit, trim look instead of making your feet look bigger.*

A polished and successful image is based on the proper fit of your clothes. Are you drowning in an oversized dress shirt, or does your slim-fit shirt pull desperately at the buttons? Are your trousers baggy, tapered, pleated, or all three? Did you polish your shoes last week or last year? These are just a few of the parameters within your control and on which colleagues will judge you. Men (and women) may not always recognize the brand another man is wearing, but it is relatively easy to tell if a coworker maintains good hygiene and takes pride in his professional appearance.

Traditionally, men have measurements they follow and styles they inherited from their fathers, brothers, bosses, or style mentors. My aim is to tell you what's in and out for *you* and help you understand the importance of looking in the mirror and identifying a proper fit so that you stay relevant and stylish as you climb the ladder of success. I'd hate for you to be sideswiped by the guy wearing the right tie just because you weren't paying attention in Fashion 101.

Let's review some of the style basics about clothing that's already hanging in your closet or can easily be purchased to update your wardrobe and help you dress to impress:

- Shirts
- Pants
- Suiting
- Sweaters and outerwear

Shirts

Does quality make a difference? Sure. But also keep your lifestyle in mind. My husband and I lead a busy life, and he loves his iron-free shirts. For these, we go to Brooks Brothers slim-fit custom shop. Online or in store, you can design to your heart's delight dress shirts that will stay wrinkle-free and can be easily maintained. Priced very closely to off-the-rack shirts, they are a great alternative. If you prefer to avoid the outrageous prices at your local dry cleaner, then iron-free material that can be maintained at home is more important than high-luxury linen. While the material should feel nice, your highest priorities should be fit, budget, and a commitment to maintaining and wearing your clothes. Just as women often do—with First Lady Michelle Obama leading the pack—men should feel free to mix high and low pieces for effortless and unique style.

When buying off the rack, check the quality of the buttons; a cross-stitch anchoring a thicker button is a good indicator of its durability. Make it a priority to get measured to ensure the perfect fit.

And, no, you cannot measure yourself. I recommend heading to a quality men's shopping destination to find out your size. (If you live near a Nordstrom, that's always a good bet.)

Style

Every ensemble involves wearing a shirt. Learn how to diversify your collection and personalize your look.

Color

I have never been in a guy's closet that doesn't have white and blue shirts. Some have only white and blue shirts...and I beg them to include more colors! Others are color hounds and wear a white or blue shirt only if a conservative situation arises. I am a big fan of blue—just vary the shades. Play around with baby blues, French (saturated or medium) blue, and every shade in between, and experiment with textures and weaves. This is the baby step before we move into patterns. Next up is white—if you love the look of a crisp, white shirt, run to your closest white shirt bar. Thomas Pink offers more than thirty styles of white shirts, making it easy to have fun with this simple classic. Add a texture like herringbone or tonal stripes for a little more style.

Adding color to your work staples will freshen your look and help you stay current. I like pinks, lavenders, stripes, and squares. Stick with lighter shades of pink and purple, and when wearing stripes keep in mind whether you will be matching them to a tie. Fine stripes are easy to wear for the everyday Joe; Bengal (medium) and butcher (medium-wide) stripes are flashier choices for the aficionado. Windowpane and square patterns are a personal favorite because they flatter most body types and come in a variety of sizes and colors. Pinpoint, twill, herringbone, hairline stripes, broken stripes, gingham, and grid styles will also help you round out your wardrobe choices.

Cuff

French or barrel? Monogrammed or left plain? Cuffs are another way to show off your unique personal style. There is a certain elegance to a cuff, and you want to be sure you choose the style that is comfortable and works for you. A button or barrel cuff is classic and perfectly appropriate in most work situations. French cuffs, which require cufflinks to secure around the wrist, are typically more formal, yet offer an opportunity to display a bit of flash for the fashion-forward gentleman. If your wrists are too skinny, cufflinks can make it appear as if you're wearing your father's shirt. If your cuff links are too big, they will look ostentatious instead of accenting your overall look.

Many of my clients wonder whether cufflinks will make them appear too slick. Historically, shirts with cufflinks were perceived as something worn only by the wealthy or for special occasions. While that stereotype has certainly changed, there is still a common misconception that wearing cufflinks—or even a nice watch—makes you appear "rich."

I meet with a lot of government contractors, politicos, and professionals who delicately walk the line between the private and public sector. My best counsel regarding this accessory (and many others) is that if you remain true to yourself, you won't look overdressed at work. Learn to dress for your audience while being mindful of your own personal and unique style. Being authentic is often admired in fashion—hence signature style statements like Hermès ties, pocket squares, tie clips, cufflinks, or even loud socks.

Mitt Romney is a great example of someone who has struggled to appear relaxed in casual clothes for years, and whose jeans and unbuttoned collars often came across as awkward to voters during the race for the White House in 2012. A costume always looks phony, and Romney was clearly more comfortable in the tailored suits and crisp ties from his private-sector days than the "working sleeves" uniform of a campaign. Authenticity trumps phoniness every time.

Button-Downs, Short-Sleeve Shirts, and Polos

When should you wear a button-down collar? First, let's define what "button-down" means—it refers to collar type. This is the most casual of dress shirts and the most formal of casual shirts. It's a choice we often see college students or the younger set make, and it's also popular for any age in academic, science, and nonprofit workplaces. This kind of shirt is not meant to be paired with a tie, due to its more casual nature; however, in any of the aforementioned industry categories, you are likely to see it with a tie and sport coat. Anytime I see a guy on the news in a button-down with a bow tie or maybe a knit tie, his uniform screams reporter, "expert," or author. Not a bad thing, but it does brand you.

The short-sleeve shirt is often paired with cotton pants in the summer and is definitely only a casual option for the office. Similarly, a polo shirt should be worn to work only on a day deemed to be that casual. Stay away from logos at the office—I have yet to write a dress code where an employer allows them at work (unless it is a company logo). Fan of the 49ers? Wear it on the weekend. And that applies even to the "nicer" one you bought for the Super Bowl luxury box you sat in with your boss (on a weekend). Striped polos are more casual than plain ones. Ideally, look for one with cuffs in the same material as the shirt—therefore, not the same polo you would wear on Saturday with the kids eating pizza.

Golf shirts are a favorite at work for many men I know. But even if you are hitting the links that day, please don't wear your golf shirt to work unless it is logo-free and blends in well enough to look like a regular shirt. Performance tops are not usually included in dress codes—not even high-end ones from your vacation at the Ritz-Carlton. Yes, there are exceptions to every rule, but try to follow this one the best you can.

Generally, the button-down, short-sleeve shirt, and polo are great for a business-casual environment, casual business travel, resort casual, or a weekend networking coffee date.

Fit

Men's shirt selections have evolved to include a variety of fits for different body shapes. Don't be intimidated by labels; try on new fits and select the one that works best.

Classic

There was a time not that long ago when most men and women thought there was only one shape of shirt for every man. The classic cut is what most men have worn throughout their professional careers. This style is cut full through the chest, waist, and armholes and has traditionally been sold at most men's retailers. Most suitable for the stocky and broad guy, it has also been worn by lean, trim, and tall guys. Now there are many newer styles to choose from, so make sure to check your options before just replenishing this traditional, oversized fit.

Style Alert: *The modern professional looks for dress shirts without a great deal of excess material in the body.*

Slim

The newest style to hit shelves and closets across America is the slim fit. Initially, this style was perceived to be for the thin or fashion-forward guy. However, with so many cuts to choose from even the athletic guy can now sport a slim-fit shirt. Each retailer or designer has its own version—from the extra-slim-fit to the trim-fit. The term does not mean the same thing at every store and some cuts are more generous than others. Proportions should flatter your physique whether you weigh one hundred and fifty or two hundred and seventy-five pounds.

Extra Slim

Don't be scared of the "extra" part! I have put men over fifty years old in extra-slim-fit shirts. It doesn't necessarily mean you look ready to hit the clubs. This style is truly suitable for both the slim guy and one who is compact and shorter. Depending on the designer of the shirt, it can work really well for the wearer who is still swimming in a trim cut or whose shoulders don't quite measure up in a slim cut. If this sounds like you, go on and try it.

Style Alert: *Even if you don't have a trim midsection, you may still be able to wear a slim-fit shirt.*

Undershirts

Whichever style of shirt you choose, make sure to assess your undershirt needs. An undershirt can be effective for absorbing sweat, covering chest hair, shoring up see-through shirts, and even offering control. I have clients who won't leave home without their Manx on for compression. Just like Spanx for women, Manx help you stand taller and suck it in. You don't have to wear undershirts to work, but if you have chest hair that protrudes from your collar or are constantly sweating, I highly recommend them. Calvin Klein makes a style with Modal and Lycra that I particularly like because it is lightweight and does not add bulk, and Banana Republic has one in pima cotton with stretch that also works well. Remember, if we can see the collar of your undershirt, make sure it is not yellowed or worn. Don't overlook this category!

Collar

A collared dress shirt should be found in almost every working man's wardrobe. And there are so many collars to choose from—a spread collar, an extreme-spread collar, a curved collar, and a button-down collar. Maybe you prefer a more academic look in a button-down collar or a more conservative point collar (very popular in the hallowed halls of D.C.). Perhaps you march down Wall Street wearing a banker's collar (white, to contrast with the shirt color) or dance to the beat of a club collar (with thinner, rounded edges). Chances are, the everyday working Joe is choosing either the popular point collar, which works well with a four-in-hand knot style, or the trendier medium-spread collar, which is wider and allows for a Windsor or half-Windsor knot.

I love how Thomas Pink, Banana Republic, Brooks Brothers, and even Men's Wearhouse design exclusive collections. Affordable style exists at every price point. And you don't need to fly to Hong Kong for a custom design. When you are out there shopping, I want to help you match your body type and face shape to the right collar style.

Spread Collars

If you have a more angular jawline, any version of the spread collar will help you seem to stand taller and even bulk you up a little (making it appear as if you go to the gym even if you don't). A wider collar broadens the torso and lends the shoulder a strong shape. I love the spread collar, because it holds the eye of your audience and keeps them engaged—great for interviews and standing presentations as well as everyday wear.

Style Alert: *Spread collars are almost universally flattering!*

Point Collars

The narrow-point collar has long been a standard style in a gentleman's shirt wardrobe. Considered by many to be the only shirt style to be worn with a tie, it is favored by the more conservative wearer and is a longtime favorite of many men in politics. However, when you choose a point collar, you are directing your audience to look down rather than up to eye level. This is not always a flattering direction. There are different versions of this collar, some narrower than others, but the direction remains the same (toward your midsection and beyond). Still, this style is great for a man with a lean physique who is testifying in court or attending a serious meeting in a conservative or traditional environment.

To any lost (fashion) sheep: be careful when choosing a trendy collar. The club collar may be "in," but it isn't for everyone. Just as a banker's collar matches the business/finance/possibly old-world job industry (picture cigars on the balcony after work), this collar style works well on the slim and young-spirited. If you don't fit the body type or emotional description of the style, wear a different shirt.

Going Custom

People often wonder, "Should I spend more than I'm accustomed to for better quality?" My main question is always, "Does it fit right, and will you wear it?" The short answer to whether you should invest in custom shirts or even a custom suit is to first analyze your body type. If you are unable to shop off the rack—maybe your shoulders are too broad or your arms too long, then custom is the way to go.

There are also a few versions of custom—you can visit a tailor to design a shirt from scratch or just to alter the length in the arms, if that is your challenge. I have quite a few clients with unique arm measurements (thirty to thirty-two inches, which is on the short side) who love shopping off the rack and have found shirts that fit in the body but just need to be shortened in the arms. Easy! Do it! Have a tailor on speed dial, or if the retailer offers tailoring, take advantage.

If you have extremely long arms, do not settle for wearing shirts with sleeves that are too short—they will not look right. I am going to repeat this, gentlemen: shirts where the cuff hits at or above the wrist bone are too short. If this is your style challenge, take it as an indicator that you cannot buy shirts off the rack and must get them custom-made. If you are wondering if this is you, remember that your shirtsleeve should extend a half an inch beyond your jacket sleeve. Similarly, if your neck size is unusual, you are probably a good candidate for custom shirts.

For the true style guy, there is no option other than custom. Time for a new suit? Off he goes to the tailor. This is not for everyone, but if you enjoy having a hand in creating and designing your clothes, custom tailoring is great. And monogramming your shirt cuff or the lining of your jacket lets the world know you are a true auteur of style.

Matching Shirts to Suits and Ties

Matching it all together is the most challenging part of the dressing process. Too many men choose to wear plain shirts or ties because they are worried about their skill in putting together a full ensemble. Once you identify the right fit for you, scale and proportion are key. The scale of the pattern on your tie can be larger or smaller than that of your shirt, but it should not be the same. Similarly, the scale of stripes or pattern on your suit or sport coat should be different from that of your shirt. For example, when you wear a large check–patterned shirt, the design or weave on your tie should be small or tight (like a dot or spot style). When you wear a finely striped shirt, choose a boldly striped tie. The juxtaposition of large and small makes both of these stylish and successful looks. See page 70 (Neckwear) for more tips.

When choosing a tie, select colors that echo those of the shirt. Prints (like paisley, dots, animals, or floral) set against stripes work well when the shades are similar but the scales differ. If you indulge in busy patterns with your shirt and tie, keep your suit or sport coat neutral. Consider polishing off your look with a pocket square. The easiest way to add this accessory to your look is to select a well-pressed white linen one, neatly folded so there is a sliver of material protruding from your outer chest suit pocket (no more than a half inch). If you want to be a little flashier, choose a patterned style or a pocket square with colored edges that coordinate with your shirt and tie. See page 72 (Pocket Squares) for more tips.

Pants

An ill-fitting shirt can be hidden underneath a jacket, but pants that are too big, too tight, too long, or too short, will always be obvious. Make sure the pants hanging in your closet match your current shape.

The Pant Front

The first thing I look for when I sift through a new client's closet are pleated pants. And you know what? I rarely find a senior executive's closet without them. My best advice: if you own them, run home and throw them out. There is usually one of two reasons you own pleated pants: you belong to a generation that believes in wearing only pleated pants, to maximize the space in the seat area, or you are so fashion-forward (and chances are you are also young) that these pants speak to you and tickle your style fancy. A third reason could be that you haven't cleaned out your closet in a long, long time.

Flat-front pants are universally flattering. They happen to be having an "in" moment now, but they will always be on my list of must-haves. Sometimes a trend comes along that is just so good it weaves itself into the history of fashion: the flat-front pant is one of those items. In fact, many men in their twenties don't know any different, while some in their sixties are still trying to come to terms with this shift in style. Pleats were once regarded as more formal than flat-front pants, but now they just look conservative or outdated, depending on the wearer (unless that wearer is tall, lean, and the "style guy" at the office). As for the "extra room in the seat" that pleats were once so fondly regarded for providing, men and designers of men's pants have adjusted their expectations and now happily meet in the middle.

Traditionally, a flat-front pant has a plain hem, while cuffs have accompanied a pleated front. The pleat-and-cuff combination draws a lot of attention to the bottom half of the wearer. The fuller cut adds the illusion of weight, and the cuffs make your legs look more compact. Cuffs are directly related to height, so if you are challenged in that department, keep in mind that cuffs will make you appear shorter. (On the opposite extreme, the extra-tall professional athlete often struggles here as well, because adding cuffs to shorten the legs will once again draw attention to them.) I simply don't recommend this style for the everyday man.

Style Alert: *If you are a size 36 waist or higher, pleated pants will make you appear bigger.*

If your closet is full of pleated, cuffed pants, you have a couple of options. One is, clearly, to go shopping. The other is to have your current pants altered, to both remove the pleats and release the cuffs. (From a style perspective, single-pleated pants can go without cuffs; double pleats should have cuffs.) If you are an average Joe, five feet eight or shorter, with a size 36 waist or higher, start alterations and hit the stores.

Style Alert: *Flat-front, plain-hem pants work on every height, weight, and physique.*

The Break

One of the most commonly asked questions from clients is, "Where should I hem my pants to create a break?" This is the dimple or soft gathering of fabric above the shoe on the front of your pants. There are three answers, depending on the look you want. The style guy may go for no break and sport the shorter-style pant that hits the top of the shoe, showing off a printed sock. The "working at my desk until 2:00 a.m." guy (you may know him as the one with stains on his tie and sleeves rolled up all the time) may go for a full break, with just a bit of bunching over the top of the shoe. The full break allows for material shrinkage but often just looks like excess fabric at the bottom of the leg. My preference is a mid-break, which ends about one inch above the top of your shoe's sole. This is neat and smart looking, and sends a neutral style message based on a good fit. The break in your pants is not the place to flex your fashion muscles.

Khaki: A Color or a Material?

The term "khakis" generally refers to the cotton variety of pants, though you will often see it as a color descriptor. These have evolved

from casual wear, to iron-free and work-appropriate. The brand Bonobos identified the gap in the market for stylish, casual pants at the
office, and I often recommend their styles to clients. Khaki-colored
pants work well paired with a casual dress shirt, brown belt, and
brown shoes, in warmer weather. During the winter months, and to
add variety to your business casual wardrobe, stock up on gray and
black iron-free dress pants (or just commit to visiting the dry cleaner
or using an iron) to pair with button-downs and sweaters, and black
accessories.

All pants are not created equal. Cotton-based khakis are different
from wool gabardine pants in a khaki color. And a wrinkle-free pant
is different from a wrinkled one. In a business-dress environment,
the best pant when you're not wearing a suit is made of gabardine. Of
course, keep climate in mind when deciding the material of your trousers. You will want a luxurious and crisp pant; in Miami, that may be a
cotton blend, while in Boston it may be wool.

The first colors to include in your dressier trouser wardrobe will be
navy and charcoal. They are great base colors that are easy to match
and work well with sport coat, shirt, and tie combinations. As you build
your professional wardrobe, add medium to light gray, tan, brown, and
black trousers to the mix. Just remember, chocolate-brown accessories
and black clothes don't match!

Suiting

The suit is the uniform of the boardroom. A wardrobe staple worn for
the past hundred years, it has certainly evolved. Despite such changes
as lapel width and number of buttons or vents, as well as changes in
industry dress codes, the suit remains the very definition of a power
ensemble. Silicon Valley dressing may work in limited environments,
but a great-looking suit will work everywhere. A suit keeps you looking
important when others don't, and it projects an aura of power. In fact,

its tireless uniform appeal is attractive to many women who mourn the day women's wear began offering so many choices!

In the last ten years the suit has evolved for many from an everyday staple to an "only when I meet with clients" ensemble. The one constant requirement is that, whether you're wearing the suit to your first interview, to a client meeting, to ring the bell on Wall Street, or to celebrate closing a deal, it *must* fit you well. The best part about our fashion climate right now is that accessible, affordable fashion is more widely available than ever, so you don't need to spend a fortune on the suit, as long as you spend a little on a good tailor. I've worked with tailors across the globe to customize suits, and I have fooled even the best of eyes with fabulous suits for $250 (I love Alfani at Macy's.) I'm not saying buy your suits at cheap-chic locations, but good quality (especially if you take care of it) is attainable on a budget. Buying a suit is an investment.

Off the Rack or Custom?

Suits are meant to be altered. Walk into the shopping experience aware that chances are very low you will be able to wear the suit you find the following day. Most high-end and luxury labels still sell suiting in the traditional manner of a "nested suit." Here, jacket and pants coordinate in size and come as a set. The hem on the pants will usually be unfinished and the jacket will need to be adjusted.

A newer style of off-the-rack suiting is suit separates. Here, you can choose items closer to your exact size. For example, you may find more precise matches to your sizing, like a 36 x 32 pant and a 44 regular jacket. (This size jacket would usually carry a 38 pant.) Suit separates are a great solution in a struggling economic climate—wonderful for new grads, job seekers, and daily suit wearers who crave variety. I often find that suit separates mirror the custom suit better than a nested suit, even though a nested suit, which typically costs more, may be made of a higher-quality fabric. And with separates, you can buy an extra pair of pants to maximize the longevity of your suit—a suggestion I often make to clients buying custom suits.

Style Alert: *Reinforce the seat of your pants to avoid a split hem and, whenever possible, purchase a second pair of pants to lengthen the life of your suit.*

If you are just starting your suit collection, begin with one navy and one gray suit in tropical-weight wool. Navy looks sharp on almost every guy and is easy to match for even the novice dresser. A plain navy suit can be versatile if you are looking to make the most of a limited wardrobe—the jacket turns into a blazer with jeans or trousers, and the pants can always be worn on their own with just a dress shirt. Your second suit should be a medium to charcoal gray—either plain or with a light pinstripe.

The trick to selecting the right kind of pinstripe is to stand about ten feet away from the mirror—if the suit looks mostly like a plain color with just a faint hint of a pinstripe, then you've nailed it! If you can really see the pinstripe, this now becomes a memorable suit—a challenge when you are working with a limited wardrobe and budget. Your overall polished image should be what your audience remembers; you don't want to be thought of as the guy who always wears the pin-striped suit.

Once you have developed your suiting wardrobe, delve into brighter pinstripes, herringbone, or colors like khaki and light gray; shades of blue, brown, or olive; and seasonal fabrics like linen and seersucker.

Fit

Whether you select a custom suit or shop for a look-alike, keep in mind a few fit guidelines.

Jacket sizes are as follows, in correspondence with your height:

Short—Up to 5'9"
Regular—5'10" to 6'
Long—6' to 6'4"
Extra Long—6'4" and up

Shoulder

The way a suit fits in the shoulder is key and will often tell you if you need to pursue a custom option. The jacket should not pull across the back, and the shoulder pads should end at your shoulders. Be sure to look in a three-way mirror and assess the situation with the tailor. If there are too many horizontal lines, your jacket is too tight; if there are too many vertical ones, it is too big.

Collar

Your jacket collar should sit flush against your dress shirt's collar, revealing one half inch of your dress shirt (collar) in the back.

Cuff

A suit jacket is traditionally meant to fit shorter in the arms than other jackets. Your shirt should show about a quarter to a half inch below the jacket cuff. This means your jacket will end at or around your wristbone.

Length

A suit jacket should end after your backside does. Typically, it should hit at the bottom of your backside, or where your knuckles land when your hands are by your sides. If it doesn't, make sure you are not mistakenly wearing a short or long.

Style Alert: *Like all rules in fashion, these rules are not hard and fast. I have put someone who is "short," at five feet eight inches, in a regular jacket instead of a short one because a style was more contemporary and better suited to his physique. And keep in mind that fits can change at different stores. Knowledge is power in creating your look!*

Vents

Jackets either come with one center vent, two side vents, or no vent. Historically, the center vent is a more casual American style, side vents an elegant English feature, and no vents Italian. When there is an option, I tend to prefer side vents because they keep a clean line on the jacket as you readjust throughout the day (from sitting to standing, moving hands in and out of pockets). Stay away from a jacket without any vents unless you chose to customize this style for your physique.

Jacket Style

Men have the option of single- or double-breasted suits. While they've both had their moments in fashion history, I lean toward the single-breasted suit. A double-breasted suit can look dapper on the right individual, but it makes most men look bigger in the midsection (or just plain old and dated). If you are taller, you can go with three buttons on the torso; otherwise, a two-button suit on which the buttons are located a bit higher than they are on the suits from the '70s is very flattering. With regard to fit, the top button on a two-button suit, or the middle button on a three-button suit, should not hit below the navel. These are also the same (and only) buttons you should close on suits.

Guidance for Going Custom

If you choose to have a suit custom-made, indulge in some of these touches to show off your investment, even if you're the only one who will appreciate these personalized features.

Lapels

Choose from a peak, notch, or shawl lapel. A wider, more angular peak offers dramatic flair, while a softer, rounded shawl is most often seen on a tuxedo. The notch lapel, with a well-defined "notch" separation between the upper and lower lapel, is standard and always stylish.

Buttons

Working buttons on the sleeves, also known as "surgeons' cuffs," are evidence of a custom suit, and a lapel buttonhole is a final flair. Opt for stitching in contrasting colors on either or both of these areas to really show off your investment. If you've gone this route, flaunt it!

Ticket pocket

A ticket pocket goes above the right hip pocket and is a signature feature many men choose to include on custom suits. You may not ever put anything in there, but the fact that you can distinguishes you from the average Joe. I like all pockets at the waist to be straight rather than curved, to minimize hips.

Lining

When that jacket gets slung over a chair at your next meeting, make a statement. Choose a lining in a bold color or fun pattern that is uniquely yours. You can also choose to line the material under the collar and, of course, have special monogramming done on the interior pocket. When I was growing up, my mom and I would include hidden messages—"I love you" or "Best Dad"—in my father's custom clothes.

Sweaters and Outerwear

In the winter, your heaviest layer may be the one your audience notices first. Whether it's the sweater you wear all day at the office, or the coat you arrive wearing to a meeting, make a positive impression.

Sweaters

If you work in a business-casual environment, sweaters may be a part of your uniform in the winter. Opt for elegant styles in wool or cashmere blends. Quarter-zip and polo styles are among the most professional and flattering options. Crew-neck and V-neck sweaters, as well as cardigans, are traditional styles that are acceptable at the office. However, they draw attention to your midsection, so avoid them if you carry extra weight. Turtlenecks can also be appropriate at the office, but beware of mock necks as they can look dated and old.

Style Alert: *Examine your sweaters every year and stop wearing to work those that are pilling, stretched out, or even slightly moth-eaten.*

Coats

Dress for the climate you live in, and save the purchase of a coat for last if you don't need it daily in cooler weather. If you will be wearing a coat to work, make sure it fits as well as your clothes (and has room underneath). I lean toward versatile styles with removable liners. Knee-length trench coats or sporty raincoats work well and match most business-casual (or dressier) attire. In the colder months, look for a winter coat that features clean lines and a simple style to avoid bulk.

Parting Thoughts

Men are lucky! You don't need to have flair to be well dressed. Choose to dress up instead of down, know your size, understand proportion, and make it a priority to look neat and polished. Maintaining a wrinkle-free, well-groomed appearance is a goal even the most style challenged fellow can attain.

WORKPLACE DOS AND DON'TS

Do avoid pants with pleats: they will give your slacks a dated look and add weight to your frame. Choose a more slimming, stylish flat-front design.

Don't force yourself to choose between comfort and class. Oxfords and loafers can combine the formality of a dress shoe and the comfort of a sneaker. Wear them for work *and* play.

Do inspect your clothes for evidence of wear and tear—unpolished shoes, frayed cuffs, and underarm stains are not professional.

Don't underestimate the importance of good grooming—make sure your routine includes a broad range of meticulous personal habits from regular haircuts to trimming fingernails.

Do match your *socks* to your *pants*—elongate your frame and stream-line your look. Matching your shoes to your belt will break up the outfit appropriately. Avoid bulky belts with gaudy embellishment.

Do look fresh and invest in iron-free shirts or a steamer, or frequent the local dry cleaner to avoid a rumpled, tired look.

Don't use your work wardrobe as an opportunity for misguided self-expression—steer clear of novelty ties, oversized jewelry, logos, and anything that attracts too much attention.

Do dress for the weather—light layers and natural, breathable fabrics will allow you to control your own temperature. Don't wear flip-flops, boat shoes, or Crocs in the summer or bulky hiking boots with a suit.

Don't overexpose yourself—tattoos and piercings should be covered at appropriate times. Don't allow wardrobe malfunctions to hurt your chances for career advancement.

4

WOMEN'S ACCESSORIES AND MEN'S FURNISHINGS

Accessories are the ultimate icebreaker. A pair of stylish shoes, interesting cuff links, or a bold piece of jewelry can spark a conversation or garner attention at an important event. Consider accessories an important finishing touch to your ensemble.

Personal encounters can demonstrate the importance of accessories at the office. Peter was sporting an Hermès tie, known to insiders as the ultimate in neckwear, the first time he met with his future boss. The senior executive, who would eventually tap Peter as a senior advisor, quickly complimented him on his tie. Fueled by the success of their first meeting, Peter wore different Hermès ties for the next couple of interviews, and the men really connected. Of course, the job offer was not based on the tie, but this tool proved an interesting advantage. In fact, a tie is a tool used by many lobbyists and bankers to connect with clients—whether it highlights shared interests or a love of couture, this accessory can be very useful. Men may sometimes believe they are appreciated only for their brainpower, but that simply isn't true.

In this chapter, we'll explore the shoe heights that work best for women in business, how to choose the right handbag to represent one's personal brand, when to invest in jewelry, and guidelines for wearing hosiery to work, as well as strategic tips for choosing assorted accessories. Men will learn the basics of matching prints, patterns, and stripes, which types of shoes are appropriate for the office, and how to shop for accessories and furnishings to wear to work.

Women's Accessories

Accessories are fun to shop for because you rarely have to undress in a fitting room, or analyze your complete look. However, your key selection of the right pair of shoes, handbag, or statement piece of jewelry can dress up or down your ensemble. Don't buy more than you need just because it's easy to shop in this category.

Shoes

Shoe shopping is a favorite pick-me-up for many women. You can always find a pair you like, they almost always fit, even when nothing else does, and the price tag (usually) doesn't break the bank. Whether you're curvy or straight, petite or tall, size 2 or 16, shoes are the universal equalizer.

The best shoes to wear to work are ones you feel comfortable and confident in all day long. Right now, too many women wear matronly flats or stylish high heels that are difficult to walk in. There are better alternatives. Rather than change from ballet flats into your "work heels" at your desk (after everyone has seen you, and chances are you've already made some lasting impressions) or ruin an outfit with comfortable yet ugly shoes, let's identify the ultimate professional shoe for you.

Heel Height

Heels more than three and half inches high may look beautiful, but they are not ideal for all-day comfort. Women are drawn to height, as if taller somehow equals skinnier. Be careful: this is really an illusion. If you are one of the few women who finds high heels more comfortable than bare feet, you might well be spotted wearing them through airport security or on a leisurely stroll at the mall. However, if high heels are part of your professional armor but they cause you pain, try a pair an inch or so lower. They will elongate your shape equally well but will be considerably more comfortable. Except in weather-appropriate situations, no one should be changing shoes in the elevator (you never know who might be riding up with you) or wearing pant lengths that don't match your commuting (*or* work) shoes. Complaining about foot pain at the office or walking in wobbly shoes is not attractive. And happy feet make a happier woman!

There is a time and place for every heel height—you just have to know when to wear it. Shoes should help reveal a message. Sky-high heels (those over four inches) don't belong at the office, high heels (three inches) can certainly be professional if you find them comfortable, and the mid-heel (between two and two and a half inches) is the average woman's perfectly professional shoe. The mid-heel is doctor-recommended for those who choose to wear heels, and they can be found in a variety of styles. A kitten heel is a personal favorite of mine; measuring between one and two inches, they look terrific with pants. These versatile low heels provide style *and* all-day comfort!

If you prefer flats, pointy-toe styles are dressiest for the office. Ballet flats have been incredibly popular for the last few years and work well in a business-casual environment, but they are hard to pair with formal business dress. If you need additional support, consider flats with a low wedge or a seven-eighths heel. A traditional penny-loafer style can also be appropriate for work, but look for dressy alternatives in patent leather or with sophisticated detailing. If you wear flats, make sure that they're a successful tool in your business image arsenal.

When I first walked into my client Lacey's closet, I was excited to see that she had a fun collection of shoes prominently displayed. I immediately spotted classic, pointy-toe, black, patent-leather pumps; playful tweed stacked heels; bright magenta kitten heels; closed-toe leopard wedges; and gold flats. Upon closer inspection, however, I identified one tiny problem: they all appeared unworn. Lacey divulged her love of shoe shopping and desperately wanted to wear her "fun" shoes, but her daily go-to was a matronly pair of square-toed, black loafers worn with cotton socks.

Lacey was shopping aspirationally, imagining a different life through her shoe choices. She regularly released her inner diva in the retail world. But once she got her purchases home, reality set in and held her back. Lacey's shoes were fabulous and exactly what she should have been wearing. At forty-one years of age, she was much too young to be trapped inside a cardboard shoebox wearing orthopedic "old lady" shoes! We put the loafers side by side with the classic, black, patent-leather pumps and compared their attributes. The loafers said, "I look old and my feet hurt," while the pumps (reasonably comfortable at two and half inches) said, "I am stylish, modern, and uncomplicated." For the first time, Lacey understood others' perception of her image—and didn't like it. Our clothing, shoes, and accessories help tell our story. Put in the effort and work hard to construct the right version.

Style Alert: *Even older professionals don't need to dress "old." Select stylish, modern flats that offer support and keep an extra bounce in your step!*

Avoid shoes that appear dressy but are made of stretch fabric, slip-on shoes with elastic on the sides, full-coverage loafers (these don't look anything like penny loafers), clunky menswear-style shoes, and chunky mules, especially when worn with socks. In fact, thick casual socks should not be worn to the office (or at least should not be visible). Try boots in the winter to cover your ankles, or opt for dressy trouser socks or knee-highs for warmth.

Sole Style

Once you identify the perfect shoe height, it's time to define fashion-forward style. While there are many classic as well as new, on-trend styles debuting every season, walking the office runway in a pair of Christian Louboutin heels will fully realize your power-shoe potential. I know women who can't wait to buy their first pair after a big promotion, and others who have been collecting styles since Carrie Bradshaw fell in love with Louboutin's shoes on "Sex in the City." They can be pointed or round, stiletto or stacked; their legendary red sole discreetly tells your audience you've made it.

The best styles for work include pointed, oval, almond, or narrowly rounded toes (see the list of stylish and comfortable shoes in chapter 7).

Any brand is acceptable, but square toes or very rounded ones offer a more casual look and can appear outdated. Either a stiletto or a stacked heel is appropriate for the office. A stiletto is skinnier (and many believe sexier); a stacked heel offers more comfort and support while still being fashion forward.

Wedges are a newer addition to the office runway and tend to be more popular in the warmer months. Black patent-leather shoes are classic and timeless, and stand up to year-round use. A nude heel that matches your skin tone will help elongate a bare leg. A pop of color in suede or leather will brighten monochromatic ensembles. Selecting shoes with a thin platform underneath the ball of the foot will add the height many women seek in a workday shoe without sacrificing comfort.

Open-Toe Shoes

If your office dress code allows for open-toe shoes, a good guideline is to wear a pair that are open in the front or the back, but not both. A sling-back or a peep-toe style mixes the seriousness of a pump and the sexiness of a sandal, without the sound effects. Don't develop a reputation at work as the woman who "clickety-clacks" down the hall! If you work in a very casual environment where your peers wear flip-flops, opt for a more professional choice, like a flat or low-wedge sandal. No matter which style you choose, a pedicure or well-groomed feet and toes are your best accessory.

Boots

During the colder months, boots are a fun addition to your work wardrobe. Whether you're shopping for ankle boots or knee-high styles, opt for simple, sleek lines and avoid anything overly chunky or bulky. Ankle boots can have a stacked, stiletto, flat, or wedge heel, and look for a pointed or round toe; avoid cowboy boots, hiking boots, or anything similar in style. Knee-high boots with dresses and skirts can be very glamorous; minimal embellishment is key. Your boots should elongate your shape—look for a fitted pull-on, or zippered style in leather or a leather and fabric combination for the ultimate in sophistication. If you work in a casual environment and want to put your boots over pants, the style must remain simple. Elaborate riding or motorcycle style boots and Uggs do not belong in an office setting.

Handbags

Your outfit does not just extend from head to toe—it also includes what you carry. Your handbag is an opportunity to continue or enhance your style statement. You've worked hard to dress effectively—don't forget to match your handbag to your leadership style.

Your handbag can communicate "tired and sloppy," "organized and prepared," or "stylish and modern" faster than you can say the words! Women often prefer not to—or forget to—invest in this pivotal style element and organizational tool. The biggest faux pas women make in this area is carrying a worn bag with straps that look ready to fall apart, or pairing extremely casual bags with business attire. Don't carry something that looks cheap, or it will distract from your professional look, and don't carry a bag more casual than your outfit. You certainly don't need to match your bag at all times, but try to match genres.

When shopping for a handbag, choose one that matches your carrying philosophy (instead of your shoes). Decide whether you are the kind of person who likes to change your bag every day or carry the same classic look for years. Be budget-savvy: rather than purchasing many cheap purses, invest in one good one. Look for a color and material that offer versatility. Black leather is certainly the most popular, though there are many options for those who prefer to avoid leather on principle. Analyze your wardrobe—if your clothing features a lot of color, a neutral bag in camel, brown, black, or a metallic shade (like pewter or bronze) will match everything. If your closet is full of neutral clothing, you can go for a statement handbag in a brighter color like red, burgundy, cobalt blue, hunter green, or eggplant. Textured or treated leathers, and embossed, patent, or glazed fabrics can also add style to an executive's neutral wardrobe. While it's okay for your bag not to match your outfit exactly, make sure it doesn't clash in style or color—don't carry a chocolate-brown bag if you wear black daily.

When selecting your preferred size, look for a bag that adds balance to your shape and weight. Small bags make you look bigger, while larger bags make you appear smaller. Will you carry your bag on your shoulder, in the crook of your elbow, or in your hand? Try putting your own stuff inside while you are in the store to make sure it fits without creating unsightly bulges. For the most flattering look, choose a bag that's the opposite of your own shape. For example, if you are very curvy, select a bag with sharp, defined lines to help add structure to your shape, like a top-handle shopper tote. If you stand tall or have angular features (like a chiseled jawline or very straight hair), an over-the-shoulder hobo style with curved edges will be flattering. You may find a bag combining two shapes; the key is to buy the one that looks good on you—not just the one you like.

The Right Price

When investing in a nice work bag to match your professional attire and overall brand message, think about the cost per wear. Don't be overwhelmed by sticker shock. An expensive-looking suit should not be paired with a $40 pleather handbag. Whereas clothing can be made to appear more expensive with tailoring and accessories, a purse by nature is a statement piece and must be chosen with care. Compare the price of a bag with the number of days you expect to carry it—a $300 bag worn every day for a year costs less than a dollar a day. Wear it for two years, and the cost drops even more!

Expect to invest in high-quality construction and to spend between $100 and $500 for your work bag. (Pleather, unless textured, doesn't look as professional and tends to deteriorate quickly.) Work-wear essential spots like Banana Republic, J.Crew, Talbots, and Ann Taylor, as well as department stores and boutiques, offer a nice selection within this price range. If you are more comfortable with the lower end of this sliding scale, scour sale racks and outlets to find a fabulous bag for less.

If you are seeking to make more of a statement with your handbag, consider a "status" or designer piece. These can go for $700 and up, depending on brand and materials. A designer bag may have a visible logo—like those by Gucci or Louis Vuitton—or it may feature a tailored, well-defined design with a brand presence that flies under the radar, like those from Marc Jacobs or Céline. Women who work in more creative industries may have a greater appreciation or interest in acquiring status bags to wow colleagues and clients, but they are relevant and effective for anyone willing to make the investment. A style faux pas for the office: fake designer bags! If you want the real thing but can't afford it, find something with a similar design aesthetic or identify your designer bag and start saving!

Style Alert: *Like clothes, bags have an expiration date. Once it looks overly worn or stained it should be tossed. If it's a hard-to-part-with status bag, move it out of your everyday closet, or visit a good cobbler or leather shop—they can often work wonders. If you have a valuable bag that simply doesn't work for you anymore, but is still in good condition, consider consigning or selling it to generate income for your next purchase.*

Organizing the Inside of Your Bag

You are at a networking event and someone asks for your business card—can you retrieve one quickly from your sleek business card holder or well-organized wallet, or are you digging through crayons, takeout menus, and hairbrushes to find one lying at the bottom of your bag? The purse journey doesn't end with the purchase of your dream bag; the inside of your bag matters, too! I often take clients shopping for handbags to teach them what styles look best with their shape and to help them learn what to expect from a handbag. A good bag should be comfortable to carry, stylish to look at, and helpful in keeping your busy life organized!

Like your closet, a handbag should *not* double as a storage container—instead, it should offer an organized way to find essentials while you're on the go. Some women like to shop for bags with numerous inside pockets, but there are alternative ways to staying organized. Make sure you can fully close your wallet (and that it's in good condition). If you save receipts, store them separately, in a small leather envelope. If you carry a multitude of savings and membership cards, place them in a separate card carrier for easy access. Do you carry makeup or hair accessories? Organize them! Gather your lipsticks or compacts and place them in a small zippered case—this makes them easy to find as well as convenient for a quick touch up. You never know when someone will get a glance inside your bag—it may be private property, but if you appear disorganized or hang on to dated, worn-out items, people will notice.

Tech Storage

If you carry a laptop, tablet, or even paper files, invest in proper storage. Books are judged by their covers—even if they shouldn't be—and so are your tech accessories! A sleeve or hard case works well for laptops and tablets, and a leather folio is a classy choice for a pad, files, or papers; these can easily slip into a bigger purse. If these items take up too much space in your handbag, you may want to consider a separate tote. If your job requires you to carry a computer daily, consider investing in a sophisticated high-end leather laptop tote or briefcase like those from Tumi. If you only need tech storage sparingly, nylon zippered totes like those from Longchamp or Kate Spade (style secret: her diaper bags make great totes!) are popular choices. You can also be eco-friendly and support causes with fabric bags, but if you're attending meetings, keep in mind that casual bags say "chic but on budget," while leather totes are more formal.

Jewelry

When it comes to wearing jewelry at the office, less is more. There may be regional and cultural differences, but, to remain professional in a corporate environment, keep noisy or ostentatious jewelry to a minimum. The best investment pieces are ones you will wear daily. Are you the kind of person who changes earrings every day? If not, small hoops, classic pearls, and diamond studs are all timeless options. Keep in mind: pink or yellow crystal studs will always look fake, and earrings longer than two inches are better saved for after-work activities.

Necklaces are a safer accessory than earrings to show off spirit and style. Here, you can easily select statement pieces to wow your audience. Long necklaces (between thirty and thirty-two inches in length) are flattering on most body types, drawing a vertical line that makes you appear slimmer; chokers tend to add weight and draw attention to your neck. A long necklace in silver or gold with circle or oval links is versatile and easy to add to many ensembles for a contemporary look. A medium-length, bold necklace (between eighteen and twenty-two inches in length) pairs well with a third piece. They are also great to wear for headshots or for television when you're framed from the shoulders up. Pearls are traditional for women but not a required purchase. If you're looking for a fresh take, select a necklace that mixes pearls with metals or fun baubles; it will stand out and look a little less conservative.

What you wear on your wrists falls into two categories: bracelets are a fun, easy-to-change accessory, while a watch should be an uncomplicated staple piece that works with everything in your closet. Most of us don't have an endless budget for accessories, so invest in a watch (if you wear one) and save on bracelets. Beware of anything too blingy—if you can see or hear it from farther than six feet away, it's too much!

Rings are perfectly appropriate for the office, but try not to wear them on more than three fingers. Ideally, select one ring-wearing finger per hand for the least amount of distraction at the office. Statement rings are fun, but avoid two-finger rings, toe rings, nose rings, or any body jewelry at the office. If you are combining real and costume jewelry—for example, engagement and wedding rings with a cocktail ring—keep in mind that you may draw a lot of attention. Opt for costume pieces that truly look "costume" so they don't get compared with what's "real."

A few of my favorite go-to spots for wear-to-work costume pieces are BaubleBar.com, CWonder.com, MaxandChloe.com, and StellaDot.com. Stand alone brands like RJ Graziano, Lauren by Ralph Lauren, Kenneth Jay Lane, House of Harlow, and Majorica can be found at department stores and on QVC or HSN. If you're ready to graduate from costume pieces, or to invest in high-quality jewelry appropriate for the office, David Yurman, Ippolita, Alexis Bitter, and Roberto Coin offer stylish wear-to-work staples.

Style Alert: *Always clean or update your jewelry once it becomes tarnished or pieces start to break.*

Hosiery

I field an incredible number of questions about the appropriateness of pantyhose at the office. A traditional accessory, and not long ago a perceived requirement for women in corporate America, the "suntanned" pair of pantyhose is officially outdated. For many, the option of a bare leg is welcome; others hope the newly styled Kate Middleton, Duchess of Cambridge, who looks flawless in perfectly matched-to-her-skin-tone hose, can help reinvigorate this sleepy style. If you choose to wear pantyhose, opt for sheer black or ultra-sheer nudes that match your skin tone in a low number denier (under 10) in a matte or shiny finish.

My client Patty, a lawyer in her late forties, not only wears pantyhose every time she goes to court, she is certain she will beat any opposing counsel who dares to show a bare leg. Clearly, there is a generation of women who believes in the power of pantyhose. Taking this position to its extreme, some women are wearing toeless panty hose with open toe shoes to work in the summer. An almost anti-style invention, this marketing gimmick offers suntanned coverage to the leg and reveals pale toes. It's a very dated look, but I know women who wear these or store them in a forgotten bottom drawer, tucked in the back for one of those "what if" moments. A shaved, well-moisturized bare leg free of bug bites and bruises *is* acceptable and stylish at most offices in a business-casual setting. But in a conservative or business-formal office, don't go bare legged until you see what senior management is wearing. Check your office dress code and your client calendar, and proceed from there. And if you're not sure what to do about pantyhose, wear pants.

Style Alert: *Dermablend leg makeup helps hide spider veins, and NARS Body Glow will make you feel like a model!*

Opaque or subtly printed tights will carry you through the colder months in style. Black tights are widely accepted with every dress code and at any age, so stock up. If you desire extra control, shop accordingly. Spanx should be a part of everyone's wardrobe. I know women who won't even leave the house in pants without a pair of capri-style Spanx "holding them in" underneath! Avoid bright tights or wide fishnet stockings. Tights in neutral colors like gray, navy, brown, or even cranberry are fashion-forward options and will add a pop of style to classic looks.

Be aware of sexiness at the office—it is one of the biggest fashion conundrums keeping senior managers up at night. At a corporate style seminar in New York, an intern courageously inquired if her casual thigh-high socks (not hose) were appropriate wear for the office. At nearly six feet tall, she found tights and pantyhose uncomfortable. Long pants were hard to find (though I quickly offered her a handy list of websites that offer pants in long sizes), and her naïve perception was that no one noticed her thigh-highs because the tops were hidden under her dress. Of course, it was my job to reveal the truth: her visible thigh-highs were not appropriate for the office. It is virtually impossible to prevent every situation in which they might be unwittingly revealed!

This story is not unusual. Many young women are unfamiliar with business fashion and continue to dress for work the way they dressed in college. Many oblivious women sit in the front row of my presentations—some have forgotten or don't like to shave their legs, while others haven't looked in a mirror to see if their hems are too short. Sit in a chair and see how far up your thigh the sun is shining! Many who wear thigh-highs don't realize that when you're seated, bent over, or even pivoting quickly, clients and coworkers see those bare thighs. Cover up, or pantyhose may become an enforced section of the dress code at your office.

Assorted Extras

Belts, wraps, and even some kinds of jewelry tend to make people nervous, so they avoid wearing these accessories. In fact, many women would trade a belt for a pin and a wrap for a scarf because those are accessories with rules they understand. However, these fashion items can be powerful outfit enhancers, and it's important to learn how to wear them properly.

Belts

Ladies, stand up! A business-appropriate belt that accentuates the professional wardrobe doesn't just go through loops on high-waisted pants; it goes up high on your natural waist. Let me show you how to find the magic spot. Lift your arms up and out. Take one hand over to the opposite side and place your thumb, and then hand, fingers spread, where your bra ends. That's your natural waist! I know it feels awkward, but this is the spot to highlight when tying a wrap dress or adding a wide elastic belt to any outfit. Whether you're short-, long-, or regular-waisted, the exact point where your rib cage curves in could be at your middle finger or a bit below your little finger. In fact, if you try on dresses already hanging in your closet, most of them probably define your waist at this same spot.

Adding a belt to your ensemble can pull it together and add a touch of sophistication. The easiest and most comfortable belt to start with is wide elastic, featuring a dressy buckle. (If your buckle is black patent, pair it with coordinating shoes for instant style.) Tie the belt around a black sheath dress and add an open blazer—the belt immediately, though subtly, highlights your waist, making you appear slimmer. (Note that the belt probably hits your waist at the same place as the top button of the blazer.) Next, try belting a monochromatic look like black pants with a coordinating shell. Add a long, ruffled, open cardi and belt it in the same place. Voilà! Your waist is highlighted rather than hidden. Adding a long necklace to this look will further elongate your figure, showing off a slender shape. Designers have been trying to create waists for years using the cut of clothes, but the reappearance of belts has finally made this feature a highlight.

Scarves and Pashminas

I have visited closets filled with bins of forgotten printed silk scarves. Many women ask if this power accessory from the 1980s and 1990s will ever come back into style. Once considered a boardroom staple, the printed silk scarf can indeed look dated today. Though some women still pull off this look beautifully, with the scarf tucked behind a popped collar on a structured blazer, it's time to sort through those bins! Keep any designer prints or favorite styles and toss the rest. Leopard is classic and fun to tie around a handbag handle, and if you find a vintage status scarf you might consider framing it to enjoy as artwork.

The stylish update to the traditional printed scarf is a pashmina scarf or oversized wrap. Both styles can be worn as a third piece to add polish and power to a business-casual ensemble. The pashmina had an "it" moment in fashion circles in the late 1990s and early 2000s, and it has since evolved into a wardrobe staple. The easiest way to wear one is over a belted dress—the wrap is loose, cozy, and glamorous all at the same time, and the belt adds structure, grounding your look. Casually throw a pashmina over your shoulders with almost any structured, fitted look. Collect an assortment of colors or patterns for a fresh seasonal take and leave a black one at the office—you never know when you might need to dress up your outfit!

Men's Furnishings

Savvy self-marketers use their accessories to generate interest. When you're in a room full of suits, your selection of accessories helps make your professional uniform unique. Adding a powerful tie, noteworthy cuff links, and stylish shoes will truly have an impact on your appearance. A designer watch is an aspirational purchase; a tie bar or even a pocket square is a high-end touch requiring less of an investment. No matter your choice of particulars, it's time to get schooled in how to polish your look and differentiate yourself from the competition.

Neckwear

Making a splash with a fantastic tie doesn't have to hit you in the wallet. Unless you are a connoisseur of designer styles, great ties are available at every price point. It can be fun to shop for loud, unusual ties, but be sure to match your ultimate selections to actual shirts, or chances are your standout pieces will be left unworn. Loud ties (bold stripes, vibrant colors) require a quiet shirt (though it can still be subtly patterned), while a softer tie (dotted or lightly patterned) demands coordination with a more powerful shirt. As explained in chapter 3, when you're matching a tie to your shirt, scale and balance are of utmost importance.

Consider changing your knot style or the width of your tie for a fresh, new look. A four-in-hand knot creates a simple, traditional look favored by many. This knot tends to be slightly asymmetrical, works well with point collars, and flatters tall, thin men. A half-Windsor knot is a more complicated style than the four-in-hand. A bit wider and more symmetrical, it pairs well with spread collars. This style is quickly becoming the new standard and looks good on most men. A full Windsor knot is arguably the most luxurious in the group as well as the most complicated to carry off—not only can it be rather large in size, it also takes up a lot of your tie's length. If you have a thicker neck, an extra-long tie is a must for this look. Also, it's good for elected officials to keep in mind that while the Windsor offers a high-end look, it's one more at home in a high-powered boardroom than in public office. The width of ties has evolved through the decades from skinny to wide; today there is a broad range available. To stay on trend, keep your tie in proportion to the lapels on your jacket. Skinny styles work best on skinny men; a medium-width tie is flattering on most men. Any tie style you select should hit at your belt buckle or a little below.

Tie storage can create a confusing mess, with fashion-forward pieces tangled up with out-of-style stinkers. Organization is important! The best way to store ties is to keep them near your shirts. Some men like to hang them on a cedar hanger or around shirts for easy dressing; others keep them rolled in a dedicated tie drawer or basket. To help preserve their shape, resist tugging your ties off; remove them the same methodical way you put them on, but in reverse. Once ties have pulls, loose threads, or stains that won't come out, it's time to let them go. With so many wonderful options out there, this natural attrition will afford you the opportunity to replenish your wardrobe with new and exciting finds.

If you favor bow ties instead of long ties, they probably figure prominently in your trademark look. Bow ties are seen as a style statement, and many daring men are remembered for this signature feature. Whereas many men these days save bow ties exclusively for tuxedos, they continue to remain an everyday favorite among educators and academics, journalists, politicians, and eccentric fashionistas. Bow ties are for those committed to the style: they showcase neck size and leave a large landscape uncovered on the chest and midsection, and thus may bring unwanted attention to those sometimes problematic areas.

Many men ask me if they can wear ties casually. Yes! I love a slightly loose and askew tie paired with a dress shirt and quarter-zip sweater. It's great for a casually dressy look that works for transitioning from the office to drinks after work. You may also choose to explore more daring color and pattern combinations, knotting preferences, tie widths, and materials.

Pocket Squares

The pocket square evolved from the handkerchief. It adds a distinctive touch of detail—and is not meant to be shared with a damsel in distress. (Carry a white hanky in your back pocket for that and other hygiene needs.) If you so desire, place a pocket square in the outer breast pocket of your jacket. Don't match it exactly to your tie; rather, choose colors from your tie-and-shirt combination. A trendsetter might pick a completely different pattern while a more conservative dresser might select finely pressed white linen, a safe and classic choice.

A shortcut to achieving this dapper style is to have a pocket square attached directly to a cardboard insert, which is simply slid into the pocket. I have had quite a few of these custom made for clients. They are great if you have a hard time getting a straight line or the perfect puff in your pocket. You can also create two- or three-point styles. Visit the fabric store to select a unique fabric, or simply add a cardboard insert to any pocket squares already in your collection. Ask a tailor to make these for you and you will never have to adjust again!

Shoes

Your shoe routine should focus on maintenance first and style second. Keep your shoes looking fresh and free of scuffs or holes. It sounds so easy, and yet many walk on in their tired, dirty shoes. With regard to style, slim is more versatile than heavy. Look for a streamlined shoe with clean lines and an oval toe box.

Although shoes can be an interesting accessory, they should blend into your overall ensemble rather than standing out or, worse, drawing negative attention. A plain-toe, premium lace-up is a stylish and sophisticated choice that matches everything in your wardrobe; it easily walks the line from business formal to dressy casual. If you prefer a visible embellishment on your shoes, opt for a perforated upper instead of a traditional cap-toe to help elongate the shape of your foot. Cap-toe styles are very popular but they direct the eye to the joint between toe and upper, shortening your foot and playing up your midsection. If you want even more of a pattern on your shoes, wing tips are a timeless choice. The style difference between the long, elegant curve of wing-tip detailing and the blunt line of the cap toe is quite noticeable.

Some men prefer slip-ons or loafers to lace-ups. With so many styles to choose from, it's perfectly appropriate to wear a pair of dressy loafers at both a power lunch and the boardroom. For a modern look, opt for loafers with a higher vamp (the top of the shoe comes closer to your ankle than your toes). Styles with a plain front, a leather strap, a penny slot, or just a touch of metal are all professional. Anything with too many buckles, like a single or double monk strap, can start to look like jewelry for your feet, so tread carefully. Continue to look for an oval toe box and avoid bulky styles with a square shape. Leather soles are always dressy, though rubber ones work well in inclement weather and with many dress codes.

As we've discussed, match your socks to your pants the best you can (select either a solid color or pattern), or make a bold fashion statement with a fun color or pattern. Do not wear thick, bulky, or faded socks to work. In addition, you might notice dressy boots being worn to the office by a trendsetter or in a business-casual environment during colder months. This is acceptable—but the boots should be professional looking.

Assorted Extras

Your overall image doesn't end with your clothing and shoes. If you carry a computer or work files, be sure to accessorize with a slim, sleek briefcase. Tech accessories, business-card holders, and wallets should not be overlooked as part of your work persona. Indulge in leather or modern tech-appropriate materials when possible. The same rules that pertain to other parts of your wardrobe apply here as well: maintain these in clean condition, and when they begin to wear, replace them!

A watch is a great tool to show off your great taste or a recent promotion. When investing in this accessory, decide whether you prefer to dress up a sporty style or dress down a fancy one. Either way, to keep your watch professional, stay away from anything too heavy or with "bling." If you're on a budget, select a simple, modern style that does not draw attention. If you wear a leather or cloth band, be sure to replace it once it becomes sweaty and smelly.

Cufflinks are a fun way to show off your personality at the office. Select a pair based on your schedule: connect with a sports-fan client or channel your inner superhero. You can be bold, funny, quirky, or a trendsetter, all with your choice of cufflinks. Tie bars (also known as tie clips) offer another way to dress up and turn heads. A classic tool for men, they have recently come back into the boardroom (no doubt helped by fashion-centric shows like *Mad Men*). The tie bar pairs well with a skinny or medium-width tie and should be placed between the third and fourth button on your shirt. (Yes, it fastens to the placket.) Finally, invest in brass collar stays. The free plastic ones that come with your shirts or from the dry cleaner are not robust enough to keep your collar standing to attention all day, week in and week out. Have fun with these accessible luxuries!

When selecting a belt, make sure it matches your shoes. Opt for a minimalist style rather than a busy one. Chunky metal buckles can draw attention to the midsection and are not as appropriate for professional dress. Smooth strap styles work nicely; textured ones add flair. Always shop for a belt one size bigger than your waist size so the buckle lands near the middle hole. Once your waist changes size and you move holes, or your belt starts to look worn out, it's time to go shopping.

Style Alert: *All of these accessories require proper maintenance!*

Eyewear for Men and Women

If you wear eyeglasses, finding the right style for your face shape is important. Try on numerous pairs to determine just the right balance and proportion. A good trick is to try a pair that is the opposite of your face shape. This works for both men and women. Look in the mirror to see where your face is broadest and most narrow. Select frames that are broad enough to balance the narrow parts but not so overwhelming that they make your face appear wider.

For example, if you have a round face, look for glasses with a square or rectangular shape. If you have a square face, look for an oval style or one with rounded, soft corners. A heart-shaped face will look good with a cat-eye style to counterbalance a narrow jawline. An oval face is easiest to match; most styles work. There are many face shapes, including hybrids of those mentioned above; what is most important is to identify whether your face is angular or more rounded.

The next step is to decide whether you want your glasses to make a bold statement or remain neutral. For frames that stand out, select plastics in the appropriate shape. This bold style will help anchor your look, adding definition to graying hair or even a bald head. Tortoise-shell, black, and textured wood are timeless styles that look good on both men and women. Colored plastic is more likely to be spotted on women, but it works for both sexes. Red, blue, or purple frames may appeal to those with flair.

If you prefer a neutral look from your glasses, opt for rimless. These are great on television (unless you're a celebrity trying to use your glasses as an accessory), because they don't draw unnecessary attention to your face or hair. If you're working with wrinkles, the rimless option also works well by helping to downplay signs of aging. It should be noted, however, that metal frames are not wrinkle-friendly.

Whichever style you select, make sure to ask for high-index lenses to avoid a Coke-bottle look and to reduce the weight of your glasses. Also, add antiglare protection if you work in bright spaces or are often photographed. If you are looking for all-in-one versatility, have your eyeglasses double as sunglasses. Transition lenses are a savvy choice for a person who frequently misplaces sunglasses, but they don't become as dark as typical sunshades. If you wear bifocals, you might want to see if your prescription will work in progressives. That way, your lenses will not have a visible line. Finally, make sure your glasses are comfortable and sit perfectly on the bridge of your nose to avoid pinching and nose marks or indentations that may bother you or temporarily detract from your look.

If you wear reading glasses, the best place to shop for them is at the grocery store, pharmacy, or airport. People tend to enjoy having multiple pairs scattered around the house or office, and it's easy to find stylish options at an affordable price point. I know several women who purchase multi-pair packs of reading glasses at the drugstore, matching colors to their outfits. If you plan to read outside, invest in tinted reading glasses to avoid that double-eyeglass look (wearing reading specs over your sunglasses,) which can age even the youngest wearer beyond their years. Maui Jim does a particularly good job at offering these hard-to-find sunglasses.

Sunglasses look good on everyone, any day of the week. You can dress them up or down, or treat them as part of a costume. Get a pair with your prescription and wear them to dodge the paparazzi or avoid a coworker at lunchtime. Save or splurge, but always shop for your face shape and make sure to select a pair with UV protection. Buy several pairs if you regularly lose your sunglasses—you always need to protect your eyes.

The last factor to consider when shopping for reading glasses or sunglasses is where to put them when you're out on the town. It can be convenient to leave your hands free by placing them on top of your head or to hang them from your shirt collar, but my personal favorite is to dangle them on a fabulous La Loop—it's a piece of jewelry with a purpose. Select a necklace style from this brand to blend into your dressy outfit, or a sporty rubberized one to match a tech-casual setting. Don't let your eyewear choices drag you down or make you look old— use this modern touch and look like a VIP.

Parting Thoughts

Fun to shop for if sometimes hard to wear, accessories help finish your look. Encourage yourself to add at least one stylish accessory to your outfit every day for a week. Before you know it, you won't even notice it anymore. Gentlemen, try pairing a striped tie with a patterned shirt or adding a pocket square to your suit. Ladies, pull out those stylish shoes hiding in your closet and add a necklace to your outfit for instant glamour. These finishing touches are sure to help get you noticed in your climb from the mailroom to the boardroom.

5
PRIMPING AND PREPPING

ow that you've learned what to wear and how to wear it, walking out the door each morning should be easier. To round out your tool kit, let's focus on overall grooming, skin care, and makeup maintenance. This is the icing on the cake! You have worked hard to get the right fit for your body type and to dress appropriately (and stylishly) for the office to ensure a professional image. Don't let sloppy beauty or grooming habits ruin your efforts.

Many senior executives have shared horror stories from the office runway with me: poorly applied makeup, uncontrollable hair, skin that can't seem to grow up, and a slew of other public problems, all the result of private negligence. Do not distract or detract from your message with chipped nail polish, dry flaky skin, electric-blue eye shadow, frizzy hair, or, if you are a man, a controllable five o'clock shadow. I will say this early so the men can relax: while you do not need to wear makeup (unless perhaps you are on TV frequently), you *do* need to read your parts of this chapter.

Unisex

Men and women have different grooming products and routines, but when it comes to skin care and body art, the guidelines are the same for everyone.

Skin Care

I'm not a doctor, cosmetologist, or any kind of skin care expert. However, I have been fortunate to work with many experts who have shared a trick or two. The most helpful lesson I learned is that to decorate your body, you need to take care of it. Good grooming leads to healthy, happy skin—something we need to make a priority. Whether you visit the dermatologist, the makeup counter, or the corner drugstore, your first step should be to neutralize your complexion. For men, the primary task is moisturizing (and yes, I will excuse your eye-roll). Just as you need to hydrate yourself (eight glasses of water daily) to stay healthy, your skin benefits from the twice-daily TLC a good moisturizer provides. The smoother your skin, the better it looks (whether you wear makeup or not).

Have you ever seen a woman with an overly "cakey" look? Most beauty bashers think this is a result of wearing too much makeup, but often it is because her skin has not been fully exfoliated or prepped to handle makeup. Breakouts, greasy skin, dry flakes, and clogged pores can all be helped by a good skin-care regimen. As with clothing, price is up to the purchaser, but here's a word of advice: a high price tag is not necessarily an indication of effectiveness. Hollywood endorses expensive new finds daily, but drugstore brands like Cetaphil and Oil of Olay have been cited by supermodels (and fashion moguls) for years for being highly effective. Experiment, find the right product for you, and then use it daily. My fitness trainer often reminds me that the best cardio equipment is the one you like to use. It's not about the specific type of machine—or the skincare brand—it's a commitment to being good to yourself.

There is so much research out there on the wonders of protecting your skin from the sun that you can hardly walk by the face-moisturizer section and find one without an SPF factor of at least 15. If you prefer plain moisturizer, consider buying a separate SPF product that goes on over or under your makeup. Even if crow's feet or forehead wrinkles aren't among your complaints (and Botox is not on your to-do list) you should be applying moisturizer with sun protection daily. Consider also investing in an under-eye cream to help hydrate, and prevent bags and dark circles; we have very few oil glands around the eyes and our skin is thinnest there. This will also help as you apply makeup—the better moisturized and maintained your skin is, the better it will hold a flawless look.

Body Art

Body art was once viewed as an absolute faux pas in the workplace, but the reality is that the face of young working Americans is changing. Literally. More and more people are decorating themselves with tattoos and piercings. At one point not so long ago, having two or three earrings in one ear was considered a deviation from the norm at work—the "extras" had to be removed before going on interviews. Now, people might bond at an interview as they share "ink" stories. What has remained the same is that while you may do what you will to your body, it cannot be a distraction in the workplace. Sure, there are plenty of sectors with more relaxed dress codes (academia, tech, fashion, creative media), but if you are under forty, you still have a few decades left to keep working and proving yourself along the way. Remove obvious body piercings that are traditionally inappropriate for work and cover up tattoos the best you can. You may have clients, investors, or just plain old bosses who hold a key to your success. Don't let knuckle tattoos be the millstone around your "suit and tie" career.

Primping for Women

The world of beauty routines, makeup essentials, and hair care can be overwhelming. If you are blessed with fabulous skin (and I know many stylish women over seventy who have never worn a drop of makeup or used a blow dryer—hi, Mom), keep doing what you are doing. But if you have blemishes or broken blood vessels, frizzy hair, hard to manage nails, or are sometimes mistaken for being older or even younger, these tips can help.

Makeup

Makeup is not just about beauty—it is a tool any woman can use to help enhance her appearance and improve her likelihood of getting hired, climbing the corporate ladder, or influencing decisions in the boardroom. In fact, in talking to human resources executives, I have received feedback that varying degrees of makeup can affect perceived trustworthiness, likability, hireability, and competence both at first glance and over time. While this might sound alarming, the reality is that a woman's appearance matters in a professional world. It is completely worth your while to cover splotchy skin, rosacea, blemishes, and under-eye circles, and to freshen up your face so it doesn't implicate its owner as an overtired, multitasking professional. We already assume that you are essentially a superhero, so there is really no need to let your heroics show so obviously in your appearance.

Makeup means something different to every woman. To some, wearing makeup means applying only foundation and mascara, which—let me be very clear—is like walking out of your house wearing only your Spanx and sunglasses. Where is the rest? Other women's makeup regimen includes only a touch of cherry ChapStick to their lips. On the other end of the spectrum, the extreme case won't even head to the grocery store without putting on her "face."

Some women apply makeup by standing right in front of a mirror (so close they could pluck their eyebrows); others apply it seated at a well-lit vanity. There isn't necessarily a right or wrong method, but be clear about why you are putting on makeup in the first place. For example, are you wearing makeup to cover up skin issues? If so, make sure you are not wearing so much that you draw attention to the wrong areas. Or do you wear makeup because you think it is expected of you as an adult working woman? If so, you may be spending an unsustainable amount of time on an activity that isn't working to your advantage. Perhaps you fall into the category of many women I know: "I only wear makeup to important meetings." Be careful if you belong to this group, because people will notice the days you do and don't wear makeup. In essence, you are signaling which days you deem important—and which ones you don't. Ideally, you want to create a skin-care and makeup routine that works for your schedule and lifestyle. For most women I work with, fifteen minutes is about it. And, ladies, that's how long men typically spend shaving, so don't gripe about making time for a makeup routine.

If makeup is your hobby or you are a beauty blogger in your spare time, enjoy adding all the "extras" to your regimen. For the rest of you, feel free to gloss over the daily use of confusing products like powder (pressed and loose), eye shadow, primers, lip liners, and highlighters. Here is a makeup regimen that works well for your face, eyes, and lips when you have only fifteen precious minutes:

Face

Step 1: Moisturize.

Step 2: Depending on the level of coverage you desire, apply a tinted moisturizer, tinted BB (beauty balm) cream, or foundation.

Step 3: Use concealer on under-eye circles, blemishes, and/or breakouts.

Step 4: Brush on bronzer to add color to your now neutral face. I like to swipe a little on the cheekbones and then draw mirror-image "3"s (forehead to nose to chin) on both sides of the face for full coverage. If you so desire, add a light touch of blush to the apples of your cheeks. Feel free to select bronzer or blush here, depending on your skin color and coverage preference.

Step 5: Step three feet back from the mirror—can you tell what you've applied? If you can still see red marks you thought were covered, or if you still appear as pale as you were before applying bronzer, go back to the appropriate step and continue the process.

Eyes

A lot of people spend time on eye shadow. *Most people at the office do not notice the intricate handiwork of your eye shadow application.* Instead, add eyeliner to the upper lid (use a pencil, crayon, or brush) to make your eyes look bigger, and apply mascara to the upper lashes, adding volume and length. Keep in mind that one swipe with the mascara wand is not enough. I repeat, one swipe is not enough. Brush the wand side to side, and up and down like a toothbrush. Do not dip the wand more than once (this introduces air into the bottle), but you must apply at least two coats for a visible effect. If your lashes clump up, wait a minute for them to dry and then clean and separate them with a spoolie (a disposable mascara wand) or a cotton swab.

Professional makeup artists may apply mascara differently, but most of us are amateurs at best. If you'd like to avoid the daily mascara grind but still want to draw attention to your eyes, use an eyelash curler or invest in individually applied fake eyelashes. I have friends and clients who love these. Go for the highest-quality lashes you can afford and you won't be able to stop staring at yourself in the mirror! In general, spend more time on your overall face than on your eyes.

Lips

If you have bothered to do everything else, make sure to add something to your lips. Color will brighten and anchor your look. If color scares you, try gloss instead. Just please don't do everything else and leave your lips blank. It's like putting on a great dress and forgetting to put on your heels (or at least stylish flats).

Once you learn how to neutralize your skin—so it looks matte and free of blemishes—this fifteen-minute routine will help you feel and look like yourself when you go to work. Time doesn't simply stand still. You have to keep up—replace clothing when it becomes worn out or your shape changes, and update your skin-care and makeup regimen as your skin evolves. If you have or develop a skin-care challenge like rosacea, be prepared to spend more time investing in the right products and learning how to use them. Just as you do when choosing the right look for your body type, take control and own this. Become an expert at camouflaging your problem areas and showing off your assets.

I first met Sally when she approached me about buying a dress for a special event. I was hosting a style seminar at Lord & Taylor in New York City, and we had so much fun gussying her up. I selected a sexy dress that immediately made her feel more confident and pretty. Sally was not a person who ordinarily enjoyed shopping; she had come to the store for assistance with shopping for her specific style needs. This made it all the more fun, as I watched her break out into what I call "the happy dance"—that moment you put something on, look in the mirror, and feel so good you just start moving! It's one of my favorite client reactions and is such a privilege to see in the fitting room. Sally was a believer after trying on only a couple of dresses. I don't think she knew she could feel so pretty so quickly, and it was an absolute delight to witness.

As we walked out of the fitting room to gather accessories, I asked Sally if she wanted to get her makeup done for the party. It's a fun way to add glamour to a special evening. I could tell that makeup was not a topic she was enthusiastic about, as is often the case when you don't know much about it—so I offered to help. We talked about her current regimen and compared those results to her desired look for later that evening. We decided a new lipstick was in order. I had also noticed, however, that Sally appeared to have persistent redness in her complexion, and now that I knew her regimen, I understood she wasn't doing anything to cover it. Many ignore rosacea, or persistent redness, but it can be relatively easy to camouflage. Visits to the dermatologist can be very helpful for more serious cases and advice on how to keep flare-ups under control, but learning basic makeup tricks can be a quick confidence booster.

The best way to reduce overall redness is by washing your face regularly and using products that are oil and fragrance free, as well as by choosing allergy-tested products that don't irritate your skin. The first step is to apply a moisturizer—often rosacea is exacerbated by sun exposure, so make sure to protect yourself by also wearing sunscreen. The second step is to use a yellow- or green-tinted foundation makeup to camouflage the redness. You can further target any individual red spots with a redness-specific concealer. I have had a lot of success with clients wearing the Redness Solutions line from Clinique—a well-kept secret, it can be purchased at Sephora and most department stores.

You may also include skincare products like serums or creams to help reduce redness. Many dermatologists sell products as well, and other proven brands include Dermablend, Kiehl's, and LaRoche Posay. If you suffer from redness in your skin, take action. You can pair any of these products with your regular makeup, or try mineral makeup if your skin is extremely sensitive.

As I walked Sally to the makeup area to select a lipstick, we made a quick stop at the Clinique counter to look at redness solutions. She mentioned wearing foundation sometimes so I offered to show her something that might work better. It turned out Sally had no idea she could actually cover up her redness. She'd thought it was something she had to live with. The happy dance she did in the cosmetics department was even more enthusiastic than the one she'd done in the fitting room!

Hair

By adulthood, you and your hair should have come to an understanding. Some women have known what to do with theirs since their teen years, others have fought their hair forever, some outsource the job with weekly blowouts, and still others just cut it all off (the "mom bob"). Whatever the case, don't make it obvious to the world that you don't know what to do with your hair. Ignorance about your hair can be perceived as a lack of self-awareness. Whether you prefer a structured or more natural look, you can always enhance your hair's appearance; there are many products and techniques that can help you manage it.

Women with curls often approach me for suggestions for hairstyles appropriate for the office. Linda, a senior litigator at her law firm, told me about a male coworker's off-the-cuff remark that only women with straight hair are taken seriously and that she should consider getting a straightening treatment. That guy clearly needs to learn some manners. Linda told me how she had fought her curls for years but upon turning fifty felt liberated by them.

Women with curls often have to cut their hair more regularly, and it definitely helps to visit a stylist with expertise in cutting curly hair. Routinely using special products will also help, but don't tame the life out of your hair. The goal is not to change what you have, but to learn how to style it. Curls are absolutely acceptable in the boardroom. Frizzy, messy hair, however, is not. Together, Linda and I examined her styling and maintenance techniques to look for ways to enhance her professional image.

The Best Professional Haircut

"What is the best professional haircut?" is a popular question, along with "Should I wear my hair long or short at the office?" Women want to know both what looks best with their face shape from a style perspective and whether a conservative office environment demands a certain hair length or style. The answer has less to do with length and more to do with style. Do you have limp, straight hair? "Almost" straight hair? Hair that's frizzy because you don't have time to deal with it? Insatiable curls that you choose to ignore? If you wear a wig, extensions, or a weave, does it look real or fake? The best professional hairstyle is one that is neat and at least somewhat current and stylish.

Long hair is acceptable, but let's define what is not: hair that you must lift up when going to the restroom is probably too long. Most hair this long is not your own, so people may think it's fake. If it is your own, then chances are fair that it's limp. Optimally, healthy long hair reaches the bust area; if it starts to get close to your belly button, it's time to schedule a cut. It's not fair, but hairstyles such as dreadlocks, sister curls, or afros—though they are increasingly accepted in the professional world—may still be frowned upon in some work environments. Corporate perceptions have a way to go to fully embrace more ethnic or even religious hairstyles. If you do choose to wear a casual or "nonconformist" hairstyle, make sure your clothing and overall style evoke a professional image.

If you wear a wig, either for fun or because of illness (see page 143 for more tips), make sure to invest in a good one. Wigs also provide style options without forcing you to commit to a specific color and cut. Many people wear them, and celebrities like Beyoncé and Kim Zolciak from the *Real Housewives of Atlanta* are never without one. Like anything else you wear, flaunt it proudly. When it comes to beauty and style habits, know when to save and where to splurge.

Genetics and hair texture have everything to do with your choices when it comes to how to wear your hair. If you are considering whether to weave or not to weave, think about this: the best style for any kind of hair is a natural, sophisticated, neat one. Invest in maintaining that image. If your hair is truly unruly, get help. Weekly blowouts may not seem accessible for your lifestyle or schedule, but they can be found for $30—I know wealthy CEOs who visit their celeb stylists for coloring their tresses but favor Hair Cuttery for blowouts. You may also want to think about taking a tutorial at a nearby hair salon or learning to use one of my favorite tools for hair novices: a hair dryer with brush attachment.

A sophisticated girlfriend taught me this do-it-yourself technique in college when she couldn't believe I didn't blow-dry my hair. I was very averse back then to any type of heating tool. She gave me one lesson and I was hooked. The very next day, I walked down the street to a Duane Reade and bought my first Conair blow-dryer with brush attachment. I have since introduced this method of blow-drying to many of my clients; it works best on someone with fairly straight or wavy hair.

Step 1: Blow-dry your hair by finger combing until your hair is mostly dry or your patience runs out. Step 2: Secure the brush attachment to the blow-dryer and brush through your hair. This helps straighten while you dry. (Depending on how smooth or tangled your hair is, you may want to run a regular brush through first to get out any knots.) Step 3: Attach a comb to the blow dryer for a flatter, straighter style. Voilà! You have worked out the kinks of "almost" straight hair and added life to limp hair! The best part is that you didn't have to learn any new maneuvers, watch a YouTube video, buy a special roller brush, or contort your arm. This technique may not be perfect, but it is easy and will work for all the people headed to work with limp, squiggly, straight hair—make the effort ladies. It does get noticed.

Style Alert: *Spend more on items that are challenging or that people see the most. If you have allergies or skin issues, invest in good facial products and save on lipstick. If your hair is weak, limp, or hard to handle, spend on outsourced maintenance or tools and save on products.*

If you are looking for extra credit, add a flat iron to your routine. To save time and help keep your locks healthy, just flat-iron the ends after you blow-dry. This keeps the volume up top and your overall look polished. Also, before using any heating tools on your hair, be sure to apply thermal protection. Check the hair-product aisle or ask your stylist for sprays and serums that help protect your hair against the heat of blow-dryers and flat irons.

Let's say that hair maintenance is not your thing. Perhaps you would rather get your hair out of your face using, say, a scrunchie? Clients have asked me, "Scrunchies are not as offensive as banana clips, so they must be okay, right?" Wrong! If you want to add an accessory to your hair, consider hair sticks (like chopsticks but smaller), decorative ponytail holders (elastics with pearls, bows, or silver or gold embellishments), or understated headbands. If you prefer that your styling to be as invisible as possible, try using hair bands the same shade as your hair to secure ponytails and buns. Bobby pins, bun holders, and other assorted "made for TV" hair accessories are created to blend in to your hair. If you are worried that elastics will leave a mark on your hair, heed this style warning: come to work in the hairstyle you expect to wear most of the day. If you wear it in the door, wear it out. Everyone would notice if you changed your outfit in the middle of the day— that's why we don't do it, barring a major accident. The same can be said for hairstyles, makeup, and shoes. The more obvious you make your hair accessory, the more attention you draw. Save your paisley-patterned scrunchies, crystal-embellished barrettes, and enormous pink hair clips for when you secure your hair to wash your face at night.

Gray Hair

Gray hair is natural and beautiful; a bottle blonde with mismatched brown eyebrows is not. Your hair texture may become more coarse as it grays, so use nourishing products to maintain healthy-looking, shiny locks. Exposed roots and bad dye jobs will make you look older than salt-and-pepper tresses. Be kind to your hair, and remember that even if you don't see the top of your head, everyone else does. And yes, people taller than you can probably see it's time to color your roots before you can. You can move your part or color your roots with a short-term spray, but once you start coloring, it's a difficult commitment to break. Be prepared to invest both your time and money.

Nails

Do you go dark or light? Long or short? Real or fake? This all depends on your style personality and the health of your nails. The most important thing to consider when it comes to nail maintenance is that they should be clean and well maintained. For some, that means weekly trips to the neighborhood manicurist; for others, using a nail clipper after showering is sufficient. Faux pas at the office include chipped nails, dirty nails, cracked skin, numerous hangnails, and overly long, fake, loudly painted nails.

Color

Color is acceptable at the office, but you must wear it confidently and neatly. Keep moisturizing those hands in the winter, ladies. Keep in mind that, even if your dress code is a casual one, your nails shouldn't be the topic everyone is talking about when you leave the room. If you feel the need to match your outfit to your nail color (daily), then the polish you chose is probably too bright for you.

Don't just randomly choose colors you like—make this a strategic decision. Try on colors before committing. Treat it like a painting decision in your home—would you throw any old color on your walls? Be tactical. Do you have a big meeting this week but also a fun personal event? Go bold. Do you love pale neutrals because they match everything, but get tired of them quickly? Add a layer of glitter on the top half of your nail for a subtle highlight. If you're devoted to wearing dark or black clothes, and enjoy color and texture, then treat your nails as an accessory. If you wear patterns daily, stay away from bold colors so they don't compete with your outfit.

If your nails chip or peel after three days, be prepared to maintain them daily if you frequently wear dark polishes. You may need to add color to tips, brush on an extra topcoat to help seal in color, or remove the color sooner than expected. Often, a lighter color is easier to maintain in an office environment, because cracks and chips are less noticeable. The world of nail colors and technology has advanced in the last few years, and the category of soak-off gel colors (like Shellac, Gelish, or OPI Axxium) may also be a good option for the person whose nails don't hold color. Gel colors often last up to two or three weeks and need to be changed only once your nail grows so much it is noticeable (or if you've begun to pick it off).

Women who spend all day in uniforms, including pharmacists, postal workers, food service professionals and medical assistants, and those who work in creative fields may belong to the privileged groups where connections with customers and clients are created, and maintained, with a unique personal style touch. Indulge in nail styles that are fun but keep them looking clean and friendly. In other industries like health care, science, or education, it may be preferable not to wear nail polish. Women who work with their hands all day or who simply don't like nail polish should still consider shaping and buffing their nails. This requires much less maintenance and is still very professional.

Length

How long should your nails be? Not long enough that you can hear them! Once your fingers start to make that clickety-clacking sound on the keyboard, your nails have grown too long to be considered professional. The other challenge here, of course, is perception. If your nails are that long, people start to wonder what's under there—dirt? Bacteria?

There is a large contingent of women who apply fake nails. The trick to making them look office appropriate is to make them resemble real nails. Keep them on the shorter side and try a wrap style that appears closer to your style of nail. Many women wear fake nails not just for appearance but because their nails are weak (or they are nail biters) and showing their real nails is not an option. But it's easy to spot fake nails. They tend to be fairly thick, and if they're kept long, that thickness may be more obvious. Whether you choose to keep your nails natural, buffed, painted, or artificial, maintain a shorter, well-shaped length (rounded or square is really a personal preference), and your audience is less likely to notice the distinction.

Toenails

Toenails tend to peek out in warmer climates or in the summer. Keep them clean and short. If you enjoy pedicures, indulge. If you don't like polish, just keep them well groomed and neat. Toenails can typically be louder in color than your fingernails, so here is a place to flex your fun muscles. However, the same guidelines used for fingers apply in terms of maintenance: anything chipped indicates a lazy summer at the beach, anything dirty indicates you don't shower, and overly long toenails set off gross-out alarms. It doesn't matter if these perceptions don't match reality—it's what people believe. Know that going in, and choose wisely. Never think that someone won't look at your toes if you are wearing open-toed shoes. Trust me, someone will be bored and won't be able to stop staring.

Body

Women have so many things to keep in mind before walking out the door to work. We have now addressed fashion basics like maintaining healthy skin-care practices, applying your makeup in fifteen minutes, admitting you need to learn to deal with your hair, and practicing simple nail etiquette. Now, let's talk briefly about even more delicate topics that HR professionals often ask me about. You might think some of these answers are fairly obvious, but questions on the appropriateness of deodorant, perfume, self-tanner, and even shaved legs keep me pretty busy!

Deodorant

Don't wear too much or too little. Too much can stain your clothing and become an indicator of insecurity. The trick? If someone were to come in for a congratulatory hug, she should not be able to smell any body odor. Perfume, perhaps. Body odor, no. How do you know if you smell? Take a whiff when you remove your clothes at night.

Some women never smell but leave wet stains in the underarm area of their shirts. This is normal. If you suffer from excessive sweating, dress in fabrics that will help minimize this (stay away from silk), wear dark colors, and dress in layers. This condition can be very embarrassing, but can also be easily remedied with a prescription from your doctor (for Drysol) or a simple, periodic procedure (Botox).

What happens when your favorite (or really any) work shirt has pit stains? I know you don't think anyone can see them if you keep your arms down or wear a jacket, but it's not acceptable to continue wearing that piece! Those yellowed areas are not invisible. You will make a move during the day that will reveal them—at the office vending machine when you reach up to make your chip selection, or when you take your jacket off in the privacy of your office because you are hot. This will inevitably be the moment when the boss walks in. You would never think of wearing a shirt with a giant bleach stain on the front or a huge rip, so why should sweat stains make the cut? They shouldn't. The guideline for pit-stained clothing: toss it. It's gross.

Perfume

The impact of scent can be huge. While it may feel sexy to smell good, keep in mind that everyone has a different interpretation of a positive smell. Scents are often linked to memories, and you don't want to find yourself part of a bad one. For example, you walk into an interview and your perfume reminds your potential employer of a past employee he fired. That is not where you want his head—you want him focused, not distracted. To be safe, when going on an interview, opt to be scent-free.

Some people love the smell of perfume but others are allergic. This means you need to be sensitive about wearing it to the office. In fact, some offices are declared scent-free environments. If you are able to wear fragrance to work, make sure to select a scent that is not offensive or bold enough to cause a migraine. You may want to consider wearing an eau de toilette—many designer perfumes make this lighter version of their most popular fragrances. My preferred methods of application, depending on the scent: give the air in front of you a good spritz and then walk into it, or add a little to your wrists and the back of your neck. This helps ensure that your audience won't be choking on your scent as you enter a room.

Self-Tanner

Self-tanner is a grooming product that often makes resurgence in the spring. Insecure about pale legs or simply searching for that summer glow, we start the hunt for creams, oils, towelettes, or any new products that have hit the market since last summer. As with nail care, hair care, and makeup, the trick here is to maintain a natural appearance. Streaky self-tanned legs scream drugstore potion instead of a vacation in Turks and Caicos.

Bronzing oil tends to moisturize while also adding sheen to your skin with flecks of bronze. Because this product is not quite a self-tanner, missing a spot is not as obvious. One of my favorite must-have products to help achieve this shimmer is Nars Body Glow. It smells like vacation and is easy to apply. This is always in my stylist's kit, and I never go on television, to a party, or to a big appearance without wearing it!

Body Hair

I'd now like to write in all caps to emphasize my message: ANYONE CHOOSING TO WEAR A SKIRT, DRESS, CAPRIS, OR ANKLE PANTS SHOULD SPORT A HAIR-FREE LEG. This may seem obvious, but trust me, it is a guideline that some do not follow. I have presented seminars at Fortune 500 companies only to find an exec in the front row wearing a great pencil skirt, a fitted white blouse, and a stylish wide belt but who is accenting her beautiful ensemble with hairy legs. This is not okay. Not okay at all. Did she forget? Is it against her culture or beliefs? Folks, the answer here does not really matter. I'm not saying you always need to shave your legs for work—that's why pants were invented. You just can't wear skirts, dresses, capris, or even ankle pants and show off a hairy leg in a professional environment. Ditto goes for hair in the underarm area. If it's against your principles to shave it, then don't show it.

Grooming for Men

A skin and grooming regimen for men can range from five to fifteen minutes depending on whether you decide to shave and trim your facial hair, or just add cologne, hair gel, and moisturizer. I frequently speak at military bases in classes for transitioning soldiers. Every month or so, a three-day career course is organized for soldiers planning to leave the military. This training includes everything from résumé writing to image consulting. After a career in the military spanning twenty years, or even one lasting only five, a brush-up on interview skills and lessons about corporate culture in the private sector can be helpful. I am always impressed at the lengths our country's most powerful employer goes to in order to teach its own the skills they need to rejoin the civilian workforce.

These groups of tall, physically fit men in uniform always bring me the most interesting questions about fashion and style. Often, these men can still fit into their suits from twenty years earlier (physical training requirements can be fierce) and want to know if they can still wear them. Depending on the cut and style of the suit, balanced with current trends, that answer is sometimes yes. Once I have a group of men talking about this topic, their level of interest and excitement increases—until we talk about wearing moisturizer with sun protection. Shaving, part of the grooming process, is innate for men, but applying moisturizer is something only their mothers or wives do. Typically, their resistance is based more on a departure from their routine than fear for their masculinity; sunscreen is seen as something to do at the beach. Luckily, by the end of the hour, most have their shopping lists in hand and are ready to hit the PX (Post Exchange, like a department store located on base).

Hair

I met Joe during a seminar at the Pentagon. He was one of those guys who gave me a bit of pushback. Bald and tall, Joe didn't think anyone ever stood close enough to him to see whether he moisturized. As we engaged and I moved closer to Joe's seat, I immediately noticed something I knew I could help him with. We discussed the merits of showers and deodorant—Joe agreed these are important. So then I asked him about the flaky, irritated skin on his scalp. He thought I was joking! After being bald for so long, Joe never thought about his head. Guys with hair often use product to style their coiffures. Those who don't have hair should moisturize. After hot days in the sun, Joe's scalp was clearly burned. I asked him if he would now feel comfortable with his current skin-care regimen during an interview. Luckily, he realized there was room for improvement.

I meet a lot of men who are balding, and they often ask my opinion on their hair. They wonder if they should own the shaved head look and stop trying to cover up their hair loss or keep the little hair they have for a more professional look. Like most of my answers, my philosophy here is simple: do what looks natural and makes you feel empowered. A comb-over is not fooling anyone. Culturally, we tend to see younger guys shaving their heads or getting a short buzz cut while older, more conservative men enjoy maintaining a hairstyle. Either way, regular hair and scalp maintenance is a necessity. If you do choose to shave your head yourself, please use a mirror. I can't tell you how many times a shaved head is accompanied by an overlooked patch in the back.

If you are on the opposite extreme and have a head full of hair, please take care of it. Don't expect that because you are lucky enough to have that mane at age fifty-five, you don't need to use a little product to control it. Get regular haircuts and maintain a professional style that matches your wardrobe. If you suffer from dandruff, stock an appropriate therapeutic shampoo for regular use. Don't leave mad-scientist hair unattended unless you're actually a mad scientist.

Facial Hair

The best advice I can offer you here: pick a style and stick to it. If you are a beard or mustache guy, trim your facial hair and keep it neat. If you like a freshly shaved look, shave daily. Scruff is en vogue, but may not be appropriate for your workplace; if you decide that it is, just be sure to maintain it. Shave around the borders and trim frequently to show your boss and coworkers that this is actually a style choice and not caveman chic. Don't come to work with bloody spots or tissue stuck to your face. And yes, people really do this. Try instead shaving-relief products like Tend Skin and Barc Bump Down Relief.

Style Alert: *Ladies, borrow your man's shaving-relief product—it will help you, too, if you suffer from shaving irritation.*

Body Hair

Once you reach a certain age (often, it's the early thirties) you may get noticeable nose hairs or wild eyebrows that need pruning. Ear hair usually makes its appearance a little later. Once you spot more than you can take care of on a whim in the morning before work, it's time to invest in a pair of tweezers and a nose-hair trimmer. Sometimes you can ask your barber to maintain these critical spots, but definitely keep an eye out for hair growth, and keep trimming. These excess hairs can be extremely distracting and offensive to others. They're easy to remove, so no excuses! Regular scissors will often work for nose hair, though a trimmer is quick and convenient. If you received one last holiday season, someone was trying to give you a hint.

Chest hair is another spot men sometimes forget to address in a professional environment. Guys, this is what undershirts are for. Please stop wearing V-neck undershirts with open-collar dress shirts—they help with perspiration, but we see your chest hair. If you are an overly hairy individual, this does not work in your favor. If you are a patchy-haired individual, this also does not work in your favor. Only if you have *no hair* (and if you wax your chest, this means you must also have no irritation) can you wear an open-collar shirt and reveal a little chest. The rest of you, please cover up. Other men don't want to see your hairy chest at work and neither do women.

Nails

This is an easy topic. The rules have not changed since your mother first cut your nails when you were a baby: keep them short and keep them clean. Translation: keep a nail clipper in the bathroom and trim your nails after showers, then file the edges smooth, if necessary. Dirty nails are acceptable only when you work with greasy products that probably stain your nail beds. Not in your job description? Then you know what to do.

Cologne and Deodorant

Corporate clients often share funny human resources stories with me. I'll never forget the time a vice president told me about interviewing a high-level candidate whose cologne was so strong it activated her allergies. Others have told me that some employees are recognized solely by the scent they leave behind in elevators on the daily ride. Your scent should not be detectable unless someone comes in close enough for a hug.

An advertising firm in San Francisco once brought me in to discuss a very delicate olfactory topic with an employee: body odor. In my experience, there are two categories men fall into when it comes to B.O.: ones who wear deodorant and have a clean appearance but don't know they also need an antiperspirant to prevent the buildup of odor-causing bacteria; and the ones who choose not to wear a dual-acting antiperspirant-deodorant because they enjoy having a "manly" smell. Yes, there really are men who believe this (and who don't live in the woods or have "fresh-air" jobs).

Jack was an entitled sort of guy. Smart and driven, he had climbed the corporate ladder quickly. He was tall and bearded, with a physique that indicated he might have been a football or rugby player at one time. When we first met, I could barely detect his "manly" smell. But as he led me to his office and I walked behind him, the scent became stronger. As we arrived in his spacious office it felt as though the air had stopped circulating.

Jack and I discussed his new role: mentoring young people at the office. A guy who had done very well for himself, he was looking forward to giving back. He had recently had some personal setbacks and challenges that had opened him up to starting a new program at the office for employees. However, Jack was surprised more people were not taking advantage of this new initiative. Little did he know, there had been numerous complaints from both men and women about the way Jack smelled and his perceived lack of professionalism. It was hard to take him, and especially his advice as a mentor, seriously.

More women sit at the helm these days, and the number of working mothers is rising, evening out the boardroom. Women often notice more details than men, and their personal grooming standards are high—the workplace is not the boy's club it once was. There may have been a time when one man could excuse another's grooming faux pas, but no longer. When you smell, either as a result of too much cologne or a naturally unpleasant odor, people will comment.

I was honest with Jack. We discussed how a person's image is, in fact, a corporate tool. The conversation naturally moved into Jack's image at the office and his grooming habits. He shared with me that he didn't wear deodorant because he felt it took away from his "manliness." I decided to try an exercise: we walked around the office floor and I had him tell me if he detected any unique odors. Did the kitchen smell like microwaved popcorn? Did the woman in the elevator have on a heavy dose of perfume? Smell plays a powerful role in connecting with people, and the most successful smell is a neutral one. Unless someone is standing less than a foot away, she should be unable to smell your aftershave, deodorant, or shampoo.

Suddenly, Jack was acutely aware of scents, and as we walked back into his office, I seized the opportunity to ask him if he thought his space had an odor. Then he finally understood why he needed to start wearing deodorant–antiperspirant, and spray his office with Febreze. Jack told me recently that his mentorship program has since been incredibly successful, and branches around the country have continued his initiative.

Parting Thoughts

You will notice that I didn't mention in this chapter the necessity of brushing your teeth. Hopefully, tooth brushing is part of your regular routine (and if it's not, at least your dentist knows about it). Usually, when our teeth feel dirty we brush—it's a reactive response. Some things come naturally. However, your skin doesn't always tell you when you need sunscreen, your eyelashes don't tell you when mascara will get you noticed, and your stray stubble doesn't indicate when you're putting people off. It's your job to think about "best practices" in your grooming habits and keep yourself looking professional at work.

6

DECIPHERING THE WORKPLACE DRESS CODE

Defining wardrobe boundaries helps provide the everyday employee with guidelines for dressing responsibly. There was a time when people would check a restaurant's dress code before getting ready—people like to fit in and be appropriate. The office environment should not be any different. You want to be you—but you want to be the best business you that you can be.

Every city has its informal dress code, and the more you understand the nuances of dressing regionally, the more control you have in the boardroom. A Silicon Valley tycoon may dress like a typical undergrad, whereas a Wall Street heavyweight may prefer a mob-style zoot suit. The vibe in the tech world tends to be much more relaxed than that in finance, though fitting in while standing out can be a challenge in either industry. Understanding "tech casual" is hard, even for players who have been in the game a long time. A work environment owned mostly by a younger generation, many of whom left college for start-ups, often has an "anti-office dress code."

Confusing, yes—especially if you've spent decades dressing up for work. But that old rule stands the test of time: dress for the job you want, not just the job you have. Before interviewing at a company, identify and understand its corporate culture. There was a time when a suit was the only appropriate uniform for either gender. Now, you'll win more points for doing your research and dressing in a style that more closely aligns itself with the company dress code. Arriving in your best version of that dress code will indicate a connection with your potential peers and can signal a powerful presence to an employer.

Dress Codes

Businesses have adopted many styles of dress over the last few years (including conflicting codes in similar industries). People have been left confused and frustrated concerning appropriate styles for the office. I often speak to large and small groups at offices, retreats, and conferences to help clarify guidelines for dressing like a modern professional. Here, you will find definitions for dress codes ranging from formal business to tech casual, plus tips on what to wear for a video interview and how to dress professionally on a business trip. We will explore the definition of daily dress codes, such as business casual, and occasion-driven ones like resort casual. In every office, there are those whose style of dress indicates they are leaders and those who appear to be waiting for leadership. How will you be perceived? The answer lies in your clothing.

Defining Business Formal

Business formal is the dress code of warriors. It was once what every office demanded: a traditionally dressy and elegant style of attire. Men wore neatly pressed suits, possibly a pair of slacks with a sport coat on a "casual" day; women were almost always in skirts, dresses, or pant-suits. The fields most likely to have a majority of employees who dress like this are law firms and financial institutions. There are, of course, others—particularly on Wall Street, in parts of the government, and at Fortune 500 consulting and accounting companies. At all but the most conservative, the definition of business formal has evolved substantially.

Today, executive business dress is often casually dressy. People dress up on days when they meet with clients and dress down more often than the occasional Friday. The primary way to identify a business-formal office is by the number of people wearing suits or jackets. Women will almost always have a third piece or a suit jacket, and men will always wear a tie (indicating that a jacket lies in wait somewhere).

If men wear suits, do women have to? Not necessarily. The biggest change we have seen in corporate fashion is that women no longer need to look like men in the boardroom. If you find yourself at a high-level meeting in a conservative environment where men will be a majority (my female clients tell me they are often the only woman in the room), your alternatives include stylish new options. You will match your environment well in a tailored black pencil skirt (fitted but not too tight), matching black shell, and power third piece, preferably in a bold shade or style that suits your coloring and personality. Add a belt to highlight your waist and accessories to dress up your look. Depending on the season or city, add tights, sheer black stockings, or a nude leg and complete the look with patent-leather slim heels.

For women, the trick to maintaining an executive appearance when not wearing a suit is to keep your style sophisticated. So many people wear suits as a uniform—many times an ill-fitting one. You will look more pulled-together and authoritative in a fabulous third piece paired with a skirt, dress, or stylish slacks than someone who is absentmindedly wearing a suit. If suits suit your dress code or simply are an appealing style, stock (and stalk) fashion-forward cuts that offer a modern take on a classic design.

Managing Business Casual

The business-casual trend debuted in the late 1990s on the West Coast and was called casual Fridays. Born from a laid-back California culture, it spread from this tech capital all over the world. Its first incarnation had women in sweater sets (people bought matching sets like candy), men in polos and casual button-downs, and almost everyone in khakis. Fast-forward a decade, and some offices have completely returned to formal business while others have gone even more casual. Recent graduates entering the workplace may not know of a business environment without jeans; the House and Senate floors, however, will probably never adjust their style to accommodate denim.

Business casual means not wearing a formal jacket. Some men may opt for a sport coat with slacks, while the younger set will often wear a dress shirt with slacks (considering a sport coat too dressy or mature). Either look can work, depending on your industry. Men can also add a tie or sweater to further dress up the look. I am often asked about cardigans for men, especially in employee-uniform settings like hotel or real estate management. A polo sweater or quarter-zip sweater (in wool or cashmere) over a dress shirt and tie is dressier than a cardigan. V-neck and crew-neck sweaters can work as well on the slimmer guy (beware: this style is quick to show off a midsection). Pair with dark slacks (black, charcoal, medium-gray, brown, and navy are good basics) or subtly patterned business pants (in a pinstripe or check). The fashion-forward dresser may also opt for a stylish vest with slacks.

For women, the interpretation of business casual is more complicated, because the options feel almost unlimited. The key is to know that, although you don't need to wear a suit, your look should not be so casual that you are mistaken for an intern. A third piece adds authority and style, while bold accessories add a final touch of flair. A dress is also a key player in this category; it is easy to wear and often needs only an accessory or belt for a finished look.

Whether your workplace lets you dress casually on Fridays, when clients aren't in the office, or only when Congress is in recess, remember this: when you dress nicely all week, don't spoil your image with a sloppy outfit on casual days. If it's easier for you to match your clothes when the style is dressier, then always dress up. Otherwise, talk around the water cooler will be about the one day you wore a tacky bright orange golf shirt with stained khakis.

Jeans at the Office

The newest addition to the business-casual dress code is jeans. In many offices across the country, this trend began as a once-a-month treat or an option for select Fridays. I even have a few corporate clients that would allow their employees to wear jeans only if the employee made a small donation to charity. When most companies extend the privilege of wearing jeans to their employees, they don't expect those employees to show up to the office in weekend-worthy, knock-around jeans. A professional look is still expected, even in denim; not any old pair of jeans will suffice. Jeans for the office should be a dark wash, hemmed to properly fit your shoes (not fashionably dragging on the floor), and free of rips, whiskering, and any other indicators that mark them as overly trendy (or old). Look for trouser-style jeans or a cut that resembles dressier pants. This office-appropriate look is available on any budget for both men and women. Leave tight or low-rise jeans (and their accompanying muffin tops) at home in the drawer, together with anything acid-washed!

Even in an office where jeans can be worn daily, keep in mind it is still *an office*. Not *your* home. Therefore, it remains a professional environment. Even if others are dressing down every day, it doesn't mean you should. Buy various styles of darker jeans and maintain a neat and stylish appearance.

Polo Shirts and Logos at the Office

In the summer, many men wear polo shirts to the office instead of dress shirts. If your dress code allows for this casual touch, it is important to consider that all polo shirts are not created equal. Polos with overly large logos or patterns that you might consider wearing on a yacht or on a Cape Cod vacation are not appropriate. Golf shirts with loud patterns or those clearly made of a sporty, moisture-wicking material are also not for the office. Invest in solid color polos without logos. J.Crew does a nice job with these. Stripes are also acceptable, but test the pattern on a friend to make sure it isn't too dizzying. T-shirts with logos are not to be worn in a business-casual environment unless specifically allowed by your company.

The Office on the Weekend

It's still the office and not your garage. Yes, you can be more casual than usual, but don't get caught wearing anything you would be embarrassed to see your boss, or your boss's boss, in. Chances are, if you're working on a weekend, others are, too. Don't be a slob. Manners don't change when you eat at McDonald's, even if you're used to the Four Seasons. The rules don't change just because the days do.

Understanding (Tech) Casual

The most casually attired offices are often those in tech-related industries or even the IT department of any given company. It's widely perceived as acceptable to dress very casually in this environment. (There are regional and sector differences, of course.) Still, even in an office where anything goes, it's possible to stand out. An authentic touch is often appreciated and can become part of a signature style.

I have a client in Silicon Valley who always ensures that our appointments include enough time for sock shopping. And not just any socks. We shop for neons, brights, bold patterns, loud argyles, and other funky and fun styles that he juxtaposes with his quietly casual (tech genius) attire. Instead of a suit, his socks are his statement of power and leadership in a room full of hoodies. Even in a casual or business-casual workplace there is a hierarchy—understand the image cues unique to that environment. The next time you have an interview at a digital enterprise, check your would-be employer's ankles!

Facebook and Google may encourage a "wear what you want" philosophy, but the reality is that most businesses do not. At the end of the day, everyone hopes to be taken seriously at the office, and if you are young and dressing young (wrinkled clothing, inappropriate hemlines, sky-high heels), you are making your inexperience obvious. I have helped clients dress to impress at AOL, *The Huffington Post*, and Microsoft, and these employees report that climbing the corporate ladder can be a challenge when faces are young and dressing styles are so casual. Face time with bloggers demands a different dress code than meetings with investors. Understand that pajamas, collegiate-style "hang-out" clothes (hoodies, worn-out jeans, sweats, and track suits) are intended for painting your apartment or gardening. They are not appropriate for even a casual work environment, tech industry or otherwise.

When the PTA or Playground Is Your Office

Workspaces and schedules have evolved over the years. You may not go to a formal office each day, but that doesn't mean you're not working. Perhaps you work from home and see clients only for meetings, lunches, or business trips. Or maybe you've recently vacated your corner office and are exploring starting your own business. Working from home, networking, volunteering, and sitting on a board all have professional elements that require an appropriate wardrobe.

When prospecting for work, be sure to leave a positive impression. Bumping into someone on the playground may not warrant a business suit (though feeling like a put-together parent helps, whatever your goals may be), but a board meeting at your child's school requires different attire, especially when it might evolve into networking.

Consider this dress-code category the most flexible and fun. It can range from casually dressy in jeans while working on your computer at Starbucks to understated elegance at a client lunch. For many who graduate to this work–life schedule, this wardrobe situation is ideal. You can buy fewer "work" pieces and focus on those you really love and plan to wear. The challenge? Not letting yourself go! You may choose to work from home in your jammies, but once you step out your door, people need to understand that you mean business.

Resort Casual

One of the most popular questions I am asked is what to wear to an out-of-town conference or corporate retreat. Often, these are resort-casual conferences in Arizona, Las Vegas, South Florida, or Southern California, and women, especially, feel pressure to look stylish while remaining appropriate. The weather is usually different from that at home, and they may be looking to network on this trip. It can be exciting yet awkward to socialize with coworkers and senior managers outside the office for a few days. Having your wardrobe sorted out before you leave will help you feel prepared and confident.

Sandy was a relative newcomer at a consulting company and was excited to be making her debut as a senior team member at a resort-casual conference in Tucson, Arizona. As a fairly conservative dresser, Sandy was planning on packing light-colored (dated) suits and floral tops—a mistake that could have cost her a positive first impression. Like tech casual, resort casual is challenging for the everyday suit-wearing exec. The underlying purpose of a resort-casual dress code in a professional setting is to "lighten" the mood and encourage a relaxed friendliness. Though it can be stressful for a "uniform" dresser to prepare for, getting comfortable in more relaxed attire can help your image in these situations. Wearing the same clothes you don for work every day but in a lighter color palette won't cut it.

Though it was time to update Sandy's overall look, I certainly didn't want to dampen her enthusiasm about her upcoming business trip on our first meeting. Instead of telling her what not to pack, I helped her review her stack of magazines and catalogues to help develop her taste, encouraging a more updated style to emerge. Once I defined resort casual for Sandy, she decided to trade her baggy floral prints for brightly colored cardigans and sheath dresses. She quickly understood that looking like a serious worker bee at a resort-casual conference might not lend itself to a positive first impression and that, instead, she could remain professional (and gain bonus points) by adhering to the clearly defined dress code.

The first parameter to figure out when packing for resort casual is weather. The second is the level of dressiness for the events of the weekend. Generally, these trips are more casual during the day, with perhaps a dressier evening of cocktails or a partners' meeting. Women should consider white pants, capris, summer fabrics like linen and cotton, casually chic work dresses, and peep-toe or other conservative open-toe shoes. Men will generally be appropriate in dressier khakis, polos, dress shirts (short or long sleeve), and a sport coat (linen is a fun fabric option to include here). If a more formal evening is included in the itinerary, a suit is appropriate, though you may wish to add colorful touches with a fun dress shirt and tie to reflect the resort mood.

Spouses may be invited to resort-casual events. Their dress code is similar, though they often have a bit more leeway to wander about in casual clothes. She may be in a maxi dress and he in tailored Bermuda shorts for sightseeing, while you're dressed for an indoor business meeting or conference gathering. If you go along as a spouse, make sure you have both day and night options. And remember: the trip, though it may be on a cruise ship or at a tropical resort, is work-related for your significant other, so it's best to keep the racier bathing suits at home. Enjoy color and be casual, stylish, and appropriate. Think back to meeting your in-laws for the first time, or imagine being with them at the beach. Don't wear anything you would be embarrassed to be seen in!

Networking and Understanding Day to Night

Countless deals are pitched and closed outside the boardroom. You never know when you might need to wine and dine clients or simply attend a networking function after work. It can be embarrassing to attend an after-work function dressed too casually.

The day-to-night transition is an important one. Evening is when clients are entertained, board meetings take place, and industry events are held, and you might be unexpectedly invited to join a work function outside of the office. Alternatively, you may be attending a performance or another such personal event requiring appropriate dress. For men, accommodating this dress code may be as easy as adding the suit jacket hanging behind your office door or the extra tie you keep in a desk drawer.

For women, transitioning to an evening event can often be more complicated, especially if you did not come to work prepared. If you have a habit of wearing a third piece, this accent will always help you look dressier. If you are planning a day-to-night outfit in advance, think about wearing one of your more festive or dressier third pieces; entertaining clients or networking in the evening invites a touch of glamour. This is also an occasion to shop the accessories section of your closet. Add a belt to your dress or jacket, or include a statement necklace, earrings, and maybe even a bracelet. Bring along an extra pair of heels or a clutch (or smaller handbag) to move your ensemble from day to night. Don't be afraid to carry along extras and add them at the end of the workday. A change of accessories and shoes coupled with a quick makeup edit—brighter lipstick and touched-up mascara—will help carry your look.

Holiday Office Party

The question of what to wear to the office holiday party comes up annually. I even have clients who choose next year's dress right after this year's party so they can be sure to get it right! It is important to stay within the boundaries of the dress code and away from an inappropriately sexy look. Impress the boss, but keep the short skirts and sky-high heels for girls' night out.

Know your venue. If your office hosts a holiday party outside the office, it is typically a dressier occasion. Cocktails and dancing in a hotel ballroom call for party frocks (stay away from plunging necklines), whereas the boss's home invites stylishly festive attire (holiday colors and glittery accent pieces). Employee or spouse, the same dress code applies. My clients want to enhance their executive presence by wearing an ensemble that says "leader," not "follower." Unfortunately, an office party can have cliques, just like high school: the overbearing admins showing too much cleavage or chest hair, the recent grads who forgot (or didn't know) to dress up, the senior staff who are too dressed up, and the women in the company who don't want to be mistaken for "party dates." Dress to impress and don't let your style be your identifier.

Style Alert: *If you don't want to invest in cocktail attire that you'll only wear once or twice, try renting a dress. RentTheRunway.com is an excellent way to keep your look current and your costs down. Reserve a dress (and accessories) and hit the holiday party circuit in style.*

Your First Interview

The first interview is an important occasion, and you should be dressing to impress. Whether job competition is fierce or you happen to be the only candidate, dress for the part you want. Do your research, understand the company culture, and dress accordingly. If the style of dress is business formal, then interview in a suit. If it's business casual every day, dress one step up. Be respectful of the interview process—you don't have the job yet! For an interview, your ensemble could range from a suit to a pants or skirt combination that features a third piece. Men have it easy here—wear a suit, and if the feeling is more casual, remove your jacket when you sit down. Keep in mind that you could be interviewed by personnel in human resources, who always dress up, or by a mid-level executive comfortable in business-casual attire. Look like a star candidate and remember that everyone should start off dressing up for a job.

In the event you are interviewing at a very casually dressed company or one with a distinct dress code—perhaps due to industry or location (Hawaii vs. NYC)—it is possible to look out of place if you are *too* dressed up. However, always be a little more formal than most of the employees. If you don't know how they dress, ask friends or visit a coffee shop nearby to see how people generally look as they walk in and out of the office. There are image considerations for any interview situation: don't show cleavage or too much leg, ensure proper grooming, and make sure your clothes look neat and presentable (free of wrinkles, rips, and stains). Most interviews are seated, so be sure to try out your outfit sitting down. For men, this means making sure that your pants are not overly wrinkled, you select nice socks (preferably ones that match your pants and are not faded or with holes), and your shoes are polished. For women wearing skirts or dresses, it means making sure the length is not too short when you sit.

If you are still in college and interviewing for your first job or internship, the same advice applies. In fact, you may have recruiters on campus looking for fresh talent. If you're planning to go from class to an interview or job fair, show respect for the process and make sure you get out of your sweats first.

Interviews via Video Chat

Technology has evolved so much that many companies don't feel the need to fly in a candidate for a first interview. Just as the Internet has changed dating, it's changed other types of meetings as well. Employers feel they can get a sense of candidates before they meet them in person. First, they scrutinize the candidates' qualifications and referrals. Once they select the top tier, they may suggest a phone interview. Here, of course, it is important to sound confident and self-assured. If you are not local, a video interview may be next.

The first thing you need to know about a video interview is that the camera will not do you any favors. Many people consider the backdrop for their interview more than their wardrobe choice. Both have something in common: you and your slice of space should appear warm and friendly. Consider a creative backdrop with bookshelves or plants instead of a bare white wall or a messy dorm room. If you are interviewing for a position in a corporate setting, a corporate dress code applies. And, of course, you should plan on doing hair, makeup, and any appropriate grooming. People tend to look paler on video, so women may want to add lip color to achieve a more commanding presence and encourage eye contact. Do this even if you are not a makeup wearer. Keep noisy jewelry in a drawer; video is very sensitive to sound.

You may not know in advance whether your interview will be aired in a conference room with various people in attendance or at a cubicle with someone wearing headphones. Be prepared for anything. As on-air media talent know, good lighting makes a world of difference. Avoid having light facing the camera; instead, face a window so the light shines on you, or place a lamp above the video camera to create a halo around your face. Expect the top three buttons of your shirt, your face, and your hair to fill your frame on camera. Busy patterns will be dizzying. White or tweed clothing for your outerwear don't work well over video chat. Stick to bold colors and a nice collar or necklace that complements your face shape. And don't forget to wear pants, in case you get called away for a moment and need to stand up!

Finally, be conscious of your body language. On video, people may pay more active attention to you than they would in person. Exude an executive presence. Sit up straight, avoid making jerky movements and gestures on camera (they are distracting and awkward), and always look into the camera when you speak. But avoid looking at the video of yourself.

Networking Coffee or Breakfast Date

These days, many people have flexible work schedules, and many work from home. I often field questions concerning what to wear when meeting a prospective client, business partner, or professional networking breakfast group. This occasion is certainly not as formal as an office visit, but it still requires a professional look. And in this setting, you may actually be judged a bit more by your appearance. Potential partners like to see if there is anything to be envious of or embarrassed by before offering to help connect you to their contacts. It is important for your visual message to be as warm and friendly as your sparkling personality. Business-casual looks are appropriate for one-on-one meetings; full business dress may be in order for an industry-group setting. The best way to identify an appropriate look is to consider where others are coming from or may be headed. People going to work after a breakfast will be more dressed up; a home-based consultant meeting you for coffee will be more casual.

Your First Day of Work

What you wear to work on your first day, and even your first week (you may not meet all the key players on the first day), may brand you for the rest of your time at the company. First impressions are strong and difficult to erase. Be appropriate, be on trend (don't dress too old or too young), and debut your best ensembles. If you noticed during the interview process that the dress code is more casual or formal than you first thought, adjust accordingly. If you need to go shopping, do so before you start. Make a fresh start in your new position and lose the ring around the collar, baggy slacks, or scuffed shoes. Don't be that person caught at her desk coloring in her heels with a black permanent marker the first day on the job. (Yes, people really do this. Sometimes, it works.) And ideally, you also won't get caught stapling the hem of your pants because it has unraveled. Avoid fashion emergencies by ditching worn clothes and debuting fresh duds the first week (or month).

Business Travel and Regional Dress Codes

Get upgraded when you travel by dressing for the row you want, not just the one you were assigned. A pleasant and stylish appearance will help you move up when it comes to business travel. You can still be comfortable, but consider wearing darker colors for a sophisticated look, and don't overlook breath mints (and makeup, if applicable). Layer items and carry a jacket or versatile wrap that can go from cozy to chic in minutes. Remember, carry totes and suitcases reflective of your brand message—they are your cubicle on the go.

Following are tips for dressing to impress in boardrooms across the country.

New York City

Black is the color of style currency in this sleek fashion capital. Pull out all the stops and be on trend with statement jewelry, belts, pocket squares, tie clips, and any other fashion-forward accessories. Keep your shoes sharp, and feel free to carry an additional pair of shoes in this walking city—to be changed into *outside* the office—or invest heavily in comfortable stylish ones. In the winter, everyone will notice your outerwear, making a coat and bag (or briefcase) important purchases. Sophisticated glamour is everywhere, status-designer items are shown off, and fashion risks are taken daily.

Boston

This historic city is more conservative than New York City and even colder. An overall preppy and traditional style reigns. While not usually at the top of any best-dressed-city list, it remains a shopping hub for New England. Because of its collegiate density (and large number of academics), there seem to be more bow ties worn here than in any other major city.

Washington, D.C.

D.C. is perhaps the most up-and-coming of major destinations in terms of stylishly dressed folks, due to the Obama effect. Preppy collegiates stroll next to well-dressed lobbyists, but busy downtown streets still have commuters in white sneakers, and executives in reserved, conservative attire. Warning: the House and Senate will probably never stop dressing up for work, and many in this locale still think black is a color to be worn only to funerals. The style quotient is rising, but the politics surrounding appropriateness never will. The retail environment in this recession-resistant city continues to grow, and there are plenty of eager shoppers.

Miami

Color, texture, and embellishment are widely accepted in this city. Women in Miami were baring their arms in the boardroom long before First Lady Michelle Obama made the style mainstream, and men here have been sporting pink and lavender dress shirts longer than in any other American city. International influence calls for chic basics instead of standard khakis, and makeup and jewelry are considered must-haves rather than options. Latin style and flair, as well as showcasing physical attributes, is admired.

Chicago

A colorful and stylish city that launched many of today's style stars (Oprah, Michelle Obama, and Tina Fey, to name a few), Chicago has a more conservative and wholesome style than New York City and a laid-back approach to fashion. Luxury goods abound in the Windy City, and denim gets dressed up quite often. The marriage of high and low style is evident as you stroll Michigan Avenue.

St. Louis

This city tends to play it safe, with American classics like khakis, button-down collars, blazers, cotton pencil skirts, and printed dresses that work well in a prevailing business-casual culture. However, there is also an eclectic style to St. Louis, and a growing number of fashionistas are bringing couture to the masses.

Dallas

In this jewel of the South, many Fortune 500 folks use the weather as their gauge and dress business casual. Style is the name of the game in

Dallas, and its diversity keeps the cowboy look at bay. Look to Houston for oil and gas execs with dressier requirements at the office.

San Francisco

This city is defined by understated elegance and laid-back luxury. Business is conducted with a confidence that overrides a formal dress code—even seasoned boardrooms may never see a suit. Well groomed and stylish, San Franciscans understand an unspoken style rooted in their own evolved definition of appropriateness.

Silicon Valley

In this high-tech capital, the dress code is dramatically different than it is in nearby San Francisco. In an area skewing significantly younger due to the high numbers of start-ups, which attract the under-thirty set, the inspired style of acceptable dress is more casual than it is anywhere else in the country. Multimillionaire techies might wear hoodies and loose jeans. Even investors may dress down (but don't underestimate their financial clout).

Southern California

Hollywood inspires an anything-goes approach to fashion. In Los Angeles, Uggs are paired with miniskirts, and trends are interpreted in a unique way. What happens on the runway can also be spotted right down the street. Southern California is a mixing bowl of fashion, combining the high fashion of New York with the bare skin of Miami to create its own version of style.

Seattle

A city that boasts the headquarters of Nordstrom, Starbucks, and Microsoft, Seattle offers a dose of well-dressed, outdoorsy style. It's a mix of laid-back tech execs riding bikes and fashion-forward designers, buyers, and stylists who make holding coffee look cool while sporting the latest rain gear.

International Dress Codes

When you're travelling abroad for business, it's important to know if you'll fit in once you reach your destination. Major cities around the world subscribe to different dress codes from those in the United States. In fact, Americans often stand out for being dressed too casually. When in doubt, dress in layers to instantly transform your look from dressy to casual. Ladies will be stylish in a versatile black dress or a dark-colored ensemble that can be paired with heels or flats, a statement necklace or classic pearls, or a blazer or wrap. Men wish to look neat and presentable in any culture. Consider dark slacks with a long-sleeve dress shirt—sleeves can be rolled, a sport coat or interesting jacket added, and driving loafers or elegant lace-ups will dress your look up or down. Whether you're visiting a city for a business meeting or moving to accept a new position, take the time to learn the culture, customs, and appropriate modes of dress.

Dress Codes by Industry

Each industry sector defines its own dressing culture. Bankers will always be dressier than techies, fashion-industry insiders will be edgier than scientists, and LA's style will always be more laid-back than New York City's. Within each industry and city, however, you can choose your style track: are you admin or executive material?

Billy was a twenty-five-year-old junior analyst who struggled with being taken seriously at the conference table. Often asked to make coffee runs, even though he'd been working at the company for three years, Billy felt he wasn't advancing as quickly as his contemporaries. He shared his story with me at a leadership conference in Boston. After I listened to his woeful tale, my first question was, "Is what you are wearing now reflective of an ensemble you would wear to work?" He replied yes, while looking down guiltily at his too-short khaki pants, black socks, and overly blousy white shirt with a button-down collar. The scruffy facial hair that looked like a sixteen-year-old kid's first beard didn't help his cause.

Not surprisingly, dressing like a kid usually results in being treated like one. I encouraged Billy to start getting his clothes tailored and to pay closer attention to detail. You don't have to understand fashion to know when something is too short or too baggy, or simply doesn't fit correctly. And sure, there are famous Doogie Howser types, fashionable teen bloggers, and whiz kids, but most of us simply don't fall into these categories.

Law, Consulting, and Accounting

In law, consulting, and accounting, expect dress to be dressy and conservative. If you are at a big firm, the way you dress will identify your role within the power pyramid, so make it hard for people to tell if you are an administrative assistant or a senior associate. Calculate the hourly rate a client would pay you—does your manner of dress reflect this? Don't make the mistake of dressing cheap when your time is not. If you're self-employed in these industries, you may be visiting clients in more casual settings, like their homes. The same general standards of appropriateness apply, but use your clothing as a tool to encourage warmth and friendliness.

Wall Street and Financial Services

Although financial folks' wardrobes are typically dressy and formal, you will often find more unique touches here than in other sectors. Wall Street style often features bankers' collars, pocket squares, and cufflinks for men, while women dress to impress in fitted power suits. There are fewer women than men working in financial services, and they tend to embrace a femininity that shines in this male-dominated industry.

Fashion, Design, and Music

These creative industries allow the left brain to blossom at the office. Expect fashion-forward, edgy, and hipster looks to meet classic couture. Self-expression and individual flair are important. Rarely does a traditional suit make an appearance, though boardrooms do abound. Black is typically the color of choice, and clothing mirroring runway trends is the norm. Trends meet fads and high mixes with low.

Public Relations, Marketing, and Advertising

These fields are corporate settings for creative people. Suits make an appearance, but don't be surprised if their styles are ripped from the runway: a shorts suit worn with heels will walk arm in arm with a linen sport coat, colorful pocket square, and white pants in the summer. Wearing color is widely accepted year-round. Often when meeting or accompanying clients, industry veterans dress professionally with an appreciation for fashion and fun.

Media and Publishing

Journalists have a code of dress unlike any other. Those who report in front of the camera must dress in a flattering, marketable style; those penning today's stories may rarely walk into a formal office. This is an industry with strong guidelines on color, fit, and style for those in the limelight and full acceptance of idiosyncrasies for the talent behind the scenes. Bizarre hours keep this dress code flexible. Executives at networks, publishing houses, and other related fields maintain a stylish standard of dress that ranges from business casual to business formal.

Sales and Real Estate

When you are on the go, you are truly a visual representation of your brand. Your purse, tote, or briefcase, and perhaps your car, constitute your "cubicle," so shop accordingly. Consider that you will be in and out throughout the day, taking out your computer, business cards, pens, or phone. What you wear is even more noticeable in the absence of a physical office and staff. Your clients will probably run the gamut in terms of dress styles due to their own schedules, but you must follow a business or business-casual dress code to maintain a professional appearance.

Technology and IT

Tech companies are the most casual of professional industries, plagued by collegiate apparel and hoodies favored by the younger generation and those wrinkled khakis with sneakers so loved by the older one. Even here, though, meetings with investors or government officials require some dressing up. And, of course, if you are part of a "casual" department, be conscious that everyone else adheres to a corporate dress code—don't stand out in ill-fitting or overly schlumpy clothes.

Science, Research, and Academia

These are often laid-back, casually attired industries. While button-down collars, bow ties, and knit ties for men and dresses with heels for women are considered "dressed up," don't get into a mismatched, sloppy rut. Good grooming habits and an understanding of Fashion 101 will serve you well as you climb the ranks. Teachers and professors are a better-dressed subset and tend to show an awareness that a neat, fresh appearance in coordination with other nonverbal cues can help them influence future leaders.

Government, Politics, and Nonprofit

The civil service tends to be buttoned-up. Here, it's always better to err on the side of caution, dressing up instead of down. Even when business casual is an option, folks in these sectors often dress up more consistently. You never know when you might run out of funding or your term might expire. When you're at the mercy of those who elected you, you need to return a level of respect through the dress code. And, naturally, you need to maintain an air of authority.

Other Industries

Certain work environments require uniforms. If you are in the medical or pharmaceutical fields, the food industry, transportation, law enforcement, or hospitality, follow your dress and uniform code and remember to maintain a polished image. Customers, patients, and guests make judgments about the professionalism of industry leaders based on the presentation of those they are working with. A level of professional dress commensurate with the quality of the service is expected. Maintaining a neat overall appearance is key, especially when in uniform or abiding by a specific dress code. Taking pride in your appearance is important whether you're an x-ray technician dressed in scrubs or a member of the honor guard, dressed in full police regalia. The uniform helps people trust and believe in you during stressful or scary times.

Parting Thoughts

Dress your business best. You wear this style of clothing five times a week, so enjoy it. Try to avoid creating envy (though some may be jealous of others arriving to work in a garbage bag). Be true to yourself, but always know you will be judged on your professional appearance. That judgment may be inconsequential, but you will never really know. Don't don anything you would be ashamed to catch yourself wearing on camera, but don't regularly outshine or out-brand the boss.

Use these dress code guidelines to help identify the norms at your place of work, and hold yourself accountable. Understanding dress codes and abiding by them is yet another way to be respectful and to show off your intelligence and dedication to a professional endeavor. Just as you know when it is culturally relevant to take off your shoes in someone's home, the same understanding can help in an office setting. Be respectful and you will be respected.

7

IDENTIFY YOUR PERFECT FIT

Fit is a key aspect of dressing to impress. If your clothing is too big, it looks sloppy, as if you were wearing your dad's blazer. If your clothing fits too tightly, it may be too revealing or reflect a poor sense of dress. Either way, these styles of dress are unflattering and certainly unappealing to coworkers, managers, and potential employers. An appropriate image starts with clothes that actually fit.

When I meet with clients, examining professional attire is the first order of business. Interestingly, I often find work clothes shoved to the side of the closet, so the same pieces are worn time and time again. You know, the black pants that get worn three times in the same week? People stick with what's comfortable and what they know (or think) works. We are creatures of habit when it comes to style.

Perhaps surprisingly, many people don't know their proper size. They are dressing for the size they used to be or wish they were, or are simply wearing whatever size is available. Shopping, whether in-store or in our own closets, is an emotional experience. Through their clothing, people explore where they've been (style star in high school), where they are now (hoping to lose ten pounds), and where they want to be (put together and simply elegant). I enjoy helping people understand their unique body types and I do all I can to prevent them from searching for sales in all the wrong places. The ideal bargain is found in your own closet—everything is (hopefully) already paid for!

Without proper direction, people can shop mindlessly at stores that feature clothes that don't work for their body type. Jamming a square peg into a round hole only causes frustration. It is important to identify your body type to best match it to the appropriate clothing lines. Vanity sizing is also important to understand—you might find yourself getting skinnier walking from one store to the next!

Just Because It Zips Doesn't Mean It Fits

"Fit" is an important word to define and clarify. Just because something buttons or zips does not mean that it fits correctly. I was in the house of a client, Beth, helping her dress for an inaugural ball in Washington, D.C., and as she called me over to zip her dress I found myself in awe that she could breathe. And I am not talking about an "Oh, it feels so good, Spanx" kind of breathing. She could zip the dress—barely—but she gained back cleavage and underarm overflow. Clearly, this was not a winning combination, especially with political and celebrity paparazzi in attendance. Beth's dress was so tight that when she sat down, she actually had a few rolls appear in the midsection. Not a sight I'd be responsible for on such a big night. It is amazing how women can sometimes overlook pain and discomfort in support of perceived beauty. Luckily, I had an additional size of the dress on hand. She looked—and felt—incredible in a larger gown. It softened her back, straightened her shoulders, and flattened her stomach. Beth is living proof of the age-old fashion mantra: just because it zips doesn't mean it fits.

In the fitting room, I don't let clients get caught up in the numbers—sizes or prices. I want to know if they genuinely like what they see in the mirror before getting into the details. If you look and feel great, size numbers become secondary. However, shopping is an emotional experience, and sometimes the number on the label can be a disappointment. This applies to men too! Just get over it. Don't be a slave to the size number. It can fluctuate even when the number on the scale doesn't.

Retailers can also make it hard for us to even know our size. In one store we are a 12 and in another an 8. We can be one size on top and another on the bottom, as well as a totally separate dress size. Combine that with PMS, menopause, or even a bad day at work and you have a recipe for a shopping meltdown.

Retailers use celebrities to endorse their brands, savvy marketing materials to keep us flipping through catalogues or clicking websites, and talented visual merchandisers to keep store floors looking fresh and inviting. It is almost impossible for the mere fashion mortal to navigate, let alone to keep up on the latest trends appropriate for their body type, age range, and coloring. It is no wonder so many women treat shopping like a chore as they get older and busier. While there are many stylish women who enjoy shopping, most of the ones I meet, interview, and work with view it as a necessary evil. They may be able to enjoy the result, but the process wreaks havoc. Honestly, I know more people than I can comfortably count who have pinned their clothes to keep them from falling down just to avoid a shopping trip (men and women), and it's not only about pinching pennies.

My client Lisa came to me because her daughter kept telling her she was tired of seeing her "cute" mom wearing dated, tapered pants. Lisa hates to shop but finds herself at the store at least once a week. Nothing ever fits, and yet she visits this particular store weekly (just to see if she can find something). The setting is comfortable, the location is nearby, and the sales associates are friendly. This, plus appealing styles of clothes, should be a winning combination—yet, on every visit Lisa comes home with ill-fitting pants. Unfortunately, the clothing at Lisa's store of choice is simply not cut for her body type.

A store that is great for apple and pear body types (apples hold their weight in their midsection, pears on the bottom) will not work for someone with a straight body type—even if the clothes are age appropriate. So the first step to identifying the perfect fit is to understand your body type. Fit is all about balance and proportion—the right clothing can hide a multitude of sins. Match your body type to the right ensemble and voilà—a waist is accentuated and belly rolls disappear!

The second step is to look in the mirror (and within yourself) and learn what to accentuate and what to camouflage. Some of us know our best features, while others are confused, keeping them hidden. Ladies, get yourselves in front of a full-length mirror. (If you don't have one, bookmark this page, and run out and buy one right away!) Check for a waist: lift your shirt and look for the curvature on the sides above your hips—if there is an indentation there, then you have something that needs to be shown off. At any size. Men, take a look—is there a slender or athletic physique hiding under layers of baggy clothing? Start buying slim-fit shirts and flat-front pants.

The third step is to shop for the body you have today instead of the one you wish you had. Aspirational shopping does not help most people lose weight. However, looking great in your proper size might encourage you not to reach for that extra donut at your next morning meeting.

Women

Figuring out your size is an exercise in science and creativity. You want to become fluent in the terminology of retailers, but you also need to understand your shape—and the myriad forms it will take over time. Here we will analyze special sizes, body types, dressing throughout pregnancy, and overcoming physical challenges.

Special Sizes

Alterations should be an expectation for almost every woman. Instead of matching shoes to the length of your pants, alter them to work with your favorite shoes. Becoming familiar with the following terms retailers use will help you shop smarter.

Short/Ankle/Petite

The term "petite" used to refer exclusively to clothing for women less than five feet four inches tall, but now many retailers label pants "ankle length" or "short" (you may see A or S on the label). This works well as an identifier not only for shorter women but also taller ones who may have a shorter inseam or may just be looking for a different length. These terms generally refer to cuts for women with a thirty-inch inseam or less. For example, one of my favorite tricks is to put a five-foot-six-inch client with a shorter leg into an ankle-length, "petite" pant—the fit is usually perfect. Similarly, when you're dressing for casual days at the office, consider a few of the premium denim brands that offer petite fits with a thirty-inch inseam—they are great for taller women with shorter inseams and longer torsos. I love dark washes from 7 for All Mankind, Joe's Jeans, Citizens of Humanity, Paige, and Not Your Daughter's Jeans.

Conversely, women who are at least five feet one inch and up to a size 12 who would typically shop in the petites section for both tops and bottoms should also consider contemporary brands, like Nanette Lepore, Milly, and Trina Turk, some of which are cut to work for this shape with a simple hem alteration. Women five feet and under will most likely need to shop for separates exclusively created for petites in length and proportion. Petite women should stay away from cuffed pants; they always create the illusion of shorter legs. Expect to alter sleeve length; off-the-rack three-quarter length sleeves may also be flattering.

Tall/Long

A woman whose inseam is from thirty-four inches to thirty-eight inches in length is considered "tall." Women who measure five feet nine inches (or possibly five feet eight inches with long legs) or taller start to feel that the leg on a pant is too short if they can't find a style in "long." At this height you either need this special size or will have to let out the hem or the cuff on pants to make them long enough. Identify retailers that offer work essentials in longs, keeping in mind that many do so exclusively online, such as Banana Republic, Gap, Ann Taylor, J.Crew, Talbots, New York and Company, Express, and Long Tall Sally.

Women up to size 12 (a few brands even up to a size 14) should also consider such contemporary brands as Theory and Elie Tahari, as well as the fashion-forward bridge label Lafayette 148. These are often cut to runway length, which is extremely long in sleeve length and pant, skirt, and dress hem. If sleeves are too short but the rest of the garment fits well, consider altering the sleeves to a three-quarter length or rolling them if they have an interesting lining or slit cuffs. Never wear clothes that appear ill-fitting or you will draw extra attention to them.

The most important quality a tall person can have when it comes to fashion is confidence. Don't hunch your shoulders and try to minimize this asset. While in most industries you may wish to avoid sky-high heels (after all, you don't want to be intimidating), don't automatically reach for flats. Follow First Lady Michelle Obama's shoe example—at five feet eleven inches, she often wears kitten heels (which are between one and two inches high).

Plus

Still often called the "Women's Department," the sizes in this area begin at 14W and can run to a 26W. While the numbers 14, 16, and even 18 overlap with regular sizes, when these numbers have a W they indicate a distinct shape. "Plus size" as defined by retailers is measured in two parameters: 14–18W are different from 14–18 regular because they are cut more generously through the hips and backside, rather than just the midsection. Anything larger than 18 is also cut this way.

Body Types

Understanding your body type will make it easier to shop for the right fit. A perfect fit is about creating symmetry and balance. Shaped like an hourglass, a woman with a "curvy" body type is balanced top to bottom, with a defined waist in the middle. Most of us aren't born like this, but it's easy to create illusions. While there are many body types, the five listed below are the most common. You can fit any of the general size categories discussed above, or any specific size, while still falling under one of the following body types:

Curvy

The traditional "hourglass" is characterized by a small waist, with bust and hips that mirror each other in size. A major challenge for those with curvy figures is concealing curves and getting a proper fit in the waist.

How to dress a curvy shape at work: A curvy woman often needs to tone down or conceal her assets at the office. Stay away from items that highlight both the bust and hips—instead, look for pieces that balance your overall shape. Don't hide your figure in boxy cuts, though—fitted styles will still work well, as long as they're fitted in the right places. Dresses can become a career staple, and a third piece that nips in at the waist will add a conservative fashion flare to a sexy shape.

Straight

This shape resembles a rectangle and is sometimes referred to as "boyish." The main challenge for straight body types is to create curves where none exist. However, many brands cut for this body type; it is the shape of many fit models (the type of models designers and pattern makers use to create their clothes for "real" women, instead of even skinnier runway models).

How to dress a straight shape at work: A woman with a straight body type needs to pay extra attention to wearing the right size and filling out items so that clothes don't appear too big or small. With fewer curves, women with this silhouette can make great use of accessories, such as belts and jewelry, to help define shape. Unlike most other shapes, a straight body type can take advantage of detailing such as texture, embellishment, interesting pockets, and stripes.

Pear

This shape is also known as a "dewdrop" and is characterized by hips that appear wider than the shoulders. Pears struggle with an upper body that is smaller than the lower body.

How to dress a pear shape at work: A woman with a pear shape will always want to dress in a manner that minimizes the lower half of the body. Wearing solids on the bottom and choosing wider pant legs (flared, trouser, or wide-leg) are effective strategies to help this silhouette appear balanced. Wear structured jackets (puff sleeves also work well) to draw attention to the shoulder, as well as thicker materials that add substance to the upper body.

Apple

Women with this shape carry their weight in the midsection and abdomen and typically have slimmer legs and arms. An apple's biggest challenge is to balance the body and minimize attention to the middle.

How to dress an apple shape at work: Women with an apple shape should avoid jackets that end near the stomach, opting instead for longer styles. Slim pants with extra-long shells or tops can elongate the torso. Most apples like to show off slender legs, however, they should also camouflage the midsection and accentuate the bust.

Inverted Triangle

The inverted triangle is a very athletic look, characterized by broader shoulders and smaller hips. The biggest challenge for someone with this body type is overcoming a top-heavy look.

How to dress an inverted triangle shape at work: Women who have an inverted triangle shape should stay away from anything oversized on top; it will accentuate their size. Instead, they should balance this shape with fitted tops, or add curves with wide-leg pants. Unlike many other body types, inverted triangles can use pockets on their pants, fashionable pleats, and cuffs to help accentuate their shape. Jackets or dresses that create the illusion of hips will also work wonders for creating proportion.

Other Terms Related to Fit

Short-waisted: This is an overall look or feeling that your waist is closer to your bust than to your hips. Officially, the measurement from armpit to waist is shorter than the one from the waist to the bottom of the backside. When you get dressed, you may often feel as if the top of you looks short and your legs long. Work on creating the illusion of a waist a little lower on your body by wearing shirts, jackets, or dresses that call attention to that area.

Long-waisted: Most people find out they are long-waisted when shopping for bathing suits. You may also find that shirts are never long enough—especially with slim-style pants. Here, the measurement from armpit to waist is longer than from the waist to the bottom of the backside. This can make your legs feel short even if you are tall. Your solutions are similar to those for pears—wearing dark solids on the bottom will help add length and thereby balance your figure.

You can be any height or body type and be short- or long-waisted.

Pregnancy and Post-Pregnancy at the Office

Many women struggle with a professional look while they are pregnant. Some may begin to show before they're ready to share the news with coworkers or management, while others prefer not to invest heavily in a wardrobe that they will wear for just a few months. (Many first-time moms-to-be are surprised at how versatile a dedicated maternity wardrobe can be over time—both pre- and post-baby.) It's important to learn how to camouflage—and show off—the bump in a work-appropriate fashion and to avoid dressing in a manner that draws unwanted attention.

Some women start to show at twelve weeks (or earlier) while others can wear their regular clothes until seventeen weeks. The first step is to choose your fashion strategy: are you concealing or revealing your bump? At first, you may wish to conceal it. Many of my clients wait until the second trimester (if possible) before informing senior management about an upcoming maternity leave. While you're dressing for the "in-between" stage (not quite showing), your best strategy are monochromatic looks in your appropriate size. You may even find pieces in your closet in stretchy fabrics that will work throughout your pregnancy. Long, blousy tops and a suitable third piece, as well as select accessories (pashminas, scarves or shawls, and long necklaces work well), will help to distract your viewers. At the beginning you may want to go up a size, but resist that urge and start investing in maternity clothes—or use a Bella Band to extend the life of your pants. When shopping for maternity, go by your pre-pregnancy size. Consult a store or brand size chart when converting to European or generic small, medium, and large sizing. Often, you can get away with buying maternity bottoms and shopping for longer, but regular-size tops (anything ruched is flattering). If your clothes are too big, people will start to suspect you either have "let yourself go" or you are pregnant. Maternity clothes are cut to fit a changing body and will be much more useful throughout your pregnancy than non-maternity wear that is simply larger. Also, your post-baby body may resolve itself in a new (and even skinnier) way, so save different-size purchases for later. If you work in an extremely casual workplace, however, you can increase versatility through leveraging weekend staples from your own closet, such as maxi dresses in the summer, and other stretch fabrics that lend themselves to your pregnant shape.

Once the bump is visible, sometime between fourteen and twenty weeks, depending on your body, dress to enhance it. Don't try to hide an obvious pregnant belly. It is unflattering, will make you appear heavier, and will cause people to misinterpret your dressing cues. If you don't want to be asked about being pregnant, then make it obvious that you are. People are nosy, so don't invite the age-old question, "Has she gained weight or is she pregnant?"

If you have the figure to wear fitted clothes while pregnant and feel confident about your body, enjoy dresses of varying styles and have fun with long tops paired with fitted trousers. If you are uncomfortable with the changes to your body and any associated weight gain, you should still dress in a manner that accentuates your pregnancy to avoid looking as if you've merely gained weight. Third pieces, especially longer ones like thigh- and knee-length open cardis and wrap jackets, will be good friends, because you can layer them over tops or dresses to hide weight in the back. Spotlight the bump in fitted clothing and dress the rest of the body to your comfort level.

Style Alert: *Traditional maternity wear features an empire waist. Embrace this look if you want to show off your bump and hide everything else. Avoid it if you want to accentuate your chic figure, and look for modern designs that mimic the cut of regular clothes.*

Foundation pieces are important; be sure to update shapewear and lingerie (bras may need to be updated three times throughout your pregnancy, and Spanx come in maternity sizes) for appropriate control and to prevent spillage and rolls at the office. The list of fashion faux pas to avoid when you're pregnant is similar to the one you should be following when you're not. Be sure not to wear revealing or sheer fabrics, and if your belly button has "popped" (completely normal), you may want to wear clothes that help flatten its appearance at work (or try Miss Oops Popper Stoppers).

You don't need many pieces to get through maternity in style at the office. Destination Maternity (which includes Pea in the Pod and Motherhood Maternity as well as leased departments of these lines at Macys, and similar ones at Kohl's and Sears), H&M, Isabella Oliver, and local maternity boutiques stock great basics, as well as fun trend pieces. Invest in the pieces you wear the most—great black pants, a versatile black dress, and shells that are long enough to flatter a growing belly. Shop your current closet for third pieces and update them as needed, keeping in mind that these will work in a post-baby wardrobe as well. Knits work better than structured pieces as your weight shifts, so you may want a selection. Here, you may go one size up, depending on where you gain weight. To keep your wardrobe looking fresh and stylish, change your jewelry and shoes often, and stick to wearing darker colors. Have fun adding to your shoe collection, but keep in mind that you may need to go up at least a half size to accommodate sore, swollen, or even growing feet that are common during pregnancy.

Post-baby dressing can also be a challenge if you are nursing or pumping at the office. Some women may run home (or downstairs to day care) to nurse; others will close their office doors or try to find a private place to pump. Either way, you will want to stock your closet with easy-to-wear, office-appropriate nursing wear and accessories. Button-front blouses, scoop necks, long nursing camis, and easy-to-maneuver dresses (like shirt dresses and wrap styles) will be great choices during this time. Be sure to have breast pads on hand to prevent unsightly stains. A pashmina or shawl will work well to provide coverage and warmth while you pump in the colder months, and all-day style at work is guaranteed.

Style Alert: *The Yummie Tummie Nursing Tank is a personal favorite. Stylish and easy to wear, this breastfeeding shapewear makes you look skinnier right after you've had a baby.*

Dressing from Diagnosis Through Recovery

Managing fashion after a life-changing injury, illness, or medical procedure is a delicate subject, and I thoroughly enjoy helping people overcome their perceived limitations. I have worked closely with men and women through breast-cancer reconstruction, limb amputation, blindness, gastric bypass surgery, and significant weight loss.

Health Issues, Debilitating Injuries, and Physical Challenges

Fashion advice for the physically challenged is noticeably absent from bookstore shelves. Our troops are returning from overseas, and many are facing the added obstacle of having suffered a debilitating injury while serving our country. I help clients who are blind learn how to organize their closets and become self-sufficient shoppers. I have even had several who are more stylish than my seeing clients. Men and women experiencing extreme weight loss and undergoing bariatric surgeries are also increasing in number. I have been called upon by both hospitals and individual patients looking to learn tips for maintaining their sanity and budget as they drop in size.

Each of these life experiences presents a similar set of challenges for individuals navigating the world of professional dress. Relearning to dress with confidence, and to see oneself as stylish, is about redefining your standards of beauty. Even the smallest tip or alteration can be life-changing. Designing a closet with tactile cues and brail labels or finding a seamstress to make modifications for clients transitioning from the uniform into civilian wear after losing a limb will help them maintain independence. While the considerations of wardrobe selection and specific dressing mechanics may differ for each client, providing guidance in this capacity has truly been a privilege for me.

Style Alert: *Two simple alterations can be made to accommodate a myriad of health issues: substituting Velcro for buttons or zippers to make dressing easier, and lining clothes to be softer for those with sensitive skin. These changes allow the wearer to maintain style during what might otherwise be a difficult time.*

Breast Cancer

Breast reconstruction surgery is one of the most common medical procedures my clients have faced. So many women continue to work or stand in the spotlight during this rigorous healing process, which often lasts twelve months. I have developed techniques to help empower women to dress in a manner that keeps inquiring minds at bay while they deal with their diagnosis in private.

I remember when one of my closest girlfriends, Danielle, told me she had been diagnosed with breast cancer. I had just had my baby boy and was a complete hormonal mess. I was visiting her and she was holding the baby when she started to cry. I had a premonition and guessed immediately that she must be sick. She had already fought off cancer twice before, but this time it was much more serious and time felt more precious. Through our tears I started laughing and said, "This is something I can help you with! We need to go shopping!" In the past, I had played the role of supportive friend, being there but never really knowing how to help. Wig consultations and hat selections were the most fashion assistance I could provide. This time, Danielle's third battle with cancer, I knew there was something else I could do to help. Danielle had opted for a double mastectomy and reconstructive surgery. I knew she had a tough year ahead of her—I had been through this process with clients too many times to count. I signed on to help Danielle keep feeling feminine and beautiful through a procedure that had the possibility of negatively altering her self-image forever.

Surviving breast cancer, like overcoming many hardships in life, is about living one day at a time. The clients I work with believe in their recovery and choose not to become reclusive in the face of a serious challenge. However, many are private people and do not wish to invite coworkers, constituents, fans, paparazzi, and media into the everyday trauma of being a cancer patient. In my experience, breast cancer is a bit different from other types of cancer (not better or worse). In addition to affecting physical health, it affects your emotional well-being and self-esteem in a fundamental way. It changes the way you see yourself as a woman. Breast cancer and the decision to remove or reconstruct their breasts can cause some to question their femininity. My role is to do my best to keep that feeling at bay and to keep a woman dressed and styled in a manner that doesn't leave any self-doubt that she remains every inch a woman.

I have worked with women who chose to have a lumpectomy or single mastectomy and need prosthetic undergarments. The key here is to understand balance and to wear clothing that does not highlight the chest, or attract undue attention to the bust, where prying eyes might discern subtle differences in shape or size. Other women have opted for double mastectomies followed by reconstructive surgery. If they want to help camouflage and draw attention away from the chest and up to the face, hair extensions or wigs with hair reaching the bust or even slightly longer will help. Whether a woman opts for immediate reconstructive surgery or has expanders in place while preparing for her surgery, long hair is a terrific tool for camouflaging breast size as it changes. Give people a beautiful mane to look at and they'll stop looking elsewhere. Many women who wear expanders are unable to reach overhead when dressing for a long period of time, and I've helped my clients find the most stylish outfits to step into. In fact, many of the tricks I use for my pregnant clients come into play when styling a client with breast cancer. Directing the eye of the audience is important—no one likes to face uncomfortable scrutiny before she is ready.

Style Alert: *Customer service friendly retailer, Nordstrom, offers prosthesis bra fittings nationwide.*

Danielle and I worked effectively to create an updated wardrobe that was comfortable and stylish, and that avoided drawing attention to the bust. After surgery, she needed loose clothing that could accommodate tubes and drains. Once she went back to work, camisoles and dresses she could step into were the key to a more comfortable recovery. We paired both with color-coordinating third pieces so that once her bust size changed it wouldn't be as noticeable. Camisoles also came in handy after Danielle's surgeries, when her new bust made bras optional. Many women struggle with the discomfort of wearing a bra when they don't need to after the cosmetic and physical changes of reconstructive breast surgery. Camisoles can help them be appropriate at the office.

Through our tears and giggles grew strength. Previously only a bargain shopper, Danielle found a new respect for the function and fashion of her clothing selections. Tricks to looking skinnier had escaped her before this ordeal—now she is a seasoned "shop for your body type" shopper! As she learned more about how to dress effectively for this stage in her life, shopping and managing her feminine image became less stressful than she could have imagined.

One year after her surgery, Danielle and I walked in the Avon Walk for Breast Cancer, and I am happy to report we had fun getting decked out in pink to strut those forty miles!

Style Alert: *Whether you're undergoing breast cancer treatments or simply appreciate high style, Chikara, www.chikaradesign.com, is a unique clothing collection that is stylish and functional. Fashion forward design features help camouflage ports, scarring, and overall unevenness.*

Hair Loss

Dealing with hair loss due to illness while working in an office environment can be very traumatic. It is important to explore hairstyle solutions and become confident with your decisions. For those with permanent hair loss, perhaps due to an autoimmune disease, a wig is the most popular style solution. If hair loss is temporary due to chemotherapy, some women choose wigs, head scarves, or even peach fuzz. There is no wrong or right style here, however, you should take the opportunity to help control the way you are perceived.

If you don't want anyone at work to know what you are going through, a wig that mirrors your own hairstyle (color and shape) will help fend off prying eyes (or at least send a signal to silence wagging tongues). On the opposite extreme, I've had a few clients enjoy wearing wigs so much that they've purchased various styles (and colors) to switch it up. If a wig doesn't work for you, try tying a scarf around your head. I encourage clients to have fun owning this decision during this trying time, so that it doesn't trigger people to treat them more delicately. I've helped clients coordinate scarves to match outfits, selected fabrics for custom scarves, and spent time showing them how to tie them (there are a lot of how-to videos on YouTube)—one of my favorite styles is a bun on the side with statement earrings. It will never be easy to lose your hair, but play with accessories until you see a happy version of *you* in the mirror—that smile will help you feel whole again.

Men

Just as women should know their body types, men, too, need to understand their physiques to be effective clothing shoppers. Many men substitute comfort for style, buying the same items again and again. Take an opportunity to assess the fit of your clothing and see whether what's currently in your closet matches your body type.

Body Types

When shopping for your shape, first stand in front of the mirror and decide which body type best matches your physique.

Slim

This shape can be lean or downright skinny. If you are on the lanky side, you want to be careful not to over-accentuate your slender physique. Add texture and color to your look, and layer items to create a substantive, streamlined effect.

Athletic

This shape is broad in the shoulders and chest but narrow through the hips. Stay away from boxy cuts so you can show off your lean shape.

Men with an athletic shape should tuck in their shirts for an elongated, clean, and professional look.

Broad

This shape can be compact or tall; it is more heavyset than the athletic body type. Broad men carry their weight in the midsection. They benefit from wearing darker colors on the bottom, wider-leg styles, and a monochromatic look, when possible, to elongate the torso. Men with broad shapes should tuck in their shirts to disguise and distract from anything extra in the midsection.

Big and Tall

Men who fall into this category should play up their height and accentuate their broad shoulders. Stripes and wide patterns will make men with this shape appear bigger, so they should stick to solids or subtle, large-format prints. Darker colors will minimize size and help to conceal the midsection. Adding a blazer or wearing a suit will help big and tall men look slimmer as well as neat and polished.

Other Terms Related to Fit

The terms just covered are those retailers use to help you shop. If you fall into one of the following categories, you should consider custom or semi-custom clothes.

Short: If you're always rolling your dress shirtsleeves because they are too long, take your shirts to the tailor. This simple alteration can be done for around $15 to $20 and will make every shirt look as if it had been made just for you. Be sure to check that the shoulder lands in the right place (on your actual shoulder and not on your arm) and that you don't have excess material on the sides. Depending on your needs, you could walk out of a store with an off-the-rack shirt that will need only minor alterations of the sleeves, or you could find out that, in order to fit your size, you need to invest in a fully custom shirt. Either way, less is more. You don't need too many shirts, but the ones you have must fit properly. Do what needs to be done!

In terms of pants, men's pants don't often come in "short," but a few brands do offer a twenty-nine-inch inseam. Buy the appropriate size when available; otherwise expect to alter the hem.

Tall: If your sleeves never reach your wrists, you may need custom shirts. In my professional experience, it is easier to find casual clothes than professional attire that works for tall men. The tie is one category of men's dress where two sizes are available—standard and long. Even luxury brand Hermès has a stylish selection of long ties, cut from the same fabrics as their standard offerings. Many of the athletes I work with often have trouble finding dressy clothes that fit. Become comfortable with custom business attire (and outerwear)—it is the best, and often the only, age-appropriate solution.

Long pants are a little easier to find for business dress than in casual wear because of unfinished hems. However, if pants are still too short, invest in custom slacks. 7 for All Mankind jeans are a go-to for clients in dressy, dark styles: they go up to a 36 inseam and a 42 waist.

How to Know When an Item Doesn't Fit

Often, clients aren't aware they are wearing the wrong size until I tell them. It's not something people simply pick up along the way, and unless a garment is inappropriately tight or way too big, someone else may not tell you. Learn to identify red flags on the following clothing basics to ensure a perfect fit.

Shirts

When the buttons are pulling (this goes for both men and women), your shirt is too tight. Period. This is not a negotiable point. For guys, if you are going for a slim-fit shirt and decide to give the extra-slim-fit a test run, take a seat to check the buttons; they may not pull while you're standing. One button pulling is one too many, either way. Also, be sure to check the armholes, shoulders, and overall blousiness of the shirt.

Ladies, when buttons pull significantly across the chest (or stomach), the shirt you are wearing is not a good fit for you. There will be times when a cami underneath will help, but as an overarching guideline, consider multiple buttons not meeting up a sign that the garment doesn't fit properly. If you are bustier and also have a midsection, button-front shirts are not the most flattering look anyway. If you are just busty, don't settle for an ill-fitting top. Shirts like The Shirt by Rochelle Behrens, created with "anti-pucker technology," will help fight the gap so many women get across the bust.

Pants

Advice for both genders: if your pants have excess material in the waist, thighs, or backside (and you are not wearing a wide-leg pant), then chances are your pants are too big. While wearing your dress pants, can you pick up the waistband, pull it away from your waist, and put in a multipack of Post-its? If so, your pants are too big!

On the flip side, if your pants don't button, you suffer from extreme muffin top, or you are uncomfortable in the waist all day, then your pants are too small. If the material is too tight across the backside or thighs, creating visible underwear lines, this is also a sign it's time to size up.

Style Alert: *Ladies, if pockets pull across your hips or create an unsightly bulge, consider altering the pants to remove the pocket and seal the seam. This is an easy fix for most drycleaners or tailors. Alternatively, look for pants without pockets or with ones that open at the top.*

Dresses and Skirts

Office-appropriate dresses and skirts are meant to skim your curves. Leave items that hug for evening time, and anything baggy should find a new home. (Adding a waist-cinching wide belt will help you extend the life of these items if you are in between sizes.) The worst look for a dress or skirt is an empty one—don't let a feminine piece hang where it should fit your curves. If you can grab a handful of fabric around your hips or waist, then an item is too big. If you have ripples of horizontal fabric from one hip to the other, it's too tight.

Coats

The most common issue I see are well-dressed men and women swimming beneath voluminous, outdated coats. Look in the mirror. Can you fit three more blazers and a sweater underneath your coat? If the answer is yes, your coat is too big. If the sleeves are too short or your coat is too tight to close, donate it so someone else can dress to impress.

Style Alert: *If you're not getting the right fit in what should be your size in any category of clothing, try to find multiples of the same item to try on. The way garments are cut at a manufacturer may not always be subject to quality control on the exact sizing.*

Shoes

There really is fashionable footwear for people who wear unusual sizes or who suffer from physical ailments. Having suffered many injuries myself, and having dressed people who have spent much of their adult lives battling foot pain, I offer my best advice: keep your options open.

Think outside the box. For example, having narrow or wide feet doesn't need to limit you to specialty shoes (even if that's what you've been wearing for years). Try new brands and styles. Doctors may recommend arch support for people with plantar fasciitis, but I have helped many find relief from ballet flats—the anti-prescription. Like clothing, some shoes run big while others run small, and not all sizes are created equal (especially when comparing European and American shoe sizes). Orthotics and comfort-branded shoes are not always the *only* answer.

Ladies, before resigning yourself to a life without stylish shoes, try a few of my best-kept shoe shopping secrets:

* Go up half a size in a pointy-toe shoe to help alleviate foot pain like plantar fasciitis or avoid a troubled bunion.
* Wear heels with a built-in platform underneath the toes to relieve pressure on the ball of the foot (or if you have a Morton's neuroma). Adding a cushioned insole will also help.
* If you have a stress fracture or broken toe, look for shoes with a thick sole for added support. Try flatforms (shoes raised off the floor on an even platform) or a medium height platform wedge.

I always keep a variety of shoe insoles, heel grips, Band-Aids, and a blister stick handy for unexpected foot and shoe challenges while shopping. If you wear an extended size (under 5 or over 11) or truly require narrow or wide shoes, try specialty local or online retailers or consider custom shoes. Websites such as Nordstrom.com, Zappos.com, Amazon.com, Shoes.com, and Marmi.com allow you to shop by size, width, and style. Nordstrom's "overs and unders" sale is legendary, and they will even help you buy mismatched shoes if your feet are different sizes.

If you suffer from foot ailments and are in search of stylish and comfortable shoes, these are widely available brands for men and women, in a variety of price points, that I recommend to clients for the office:

* Allen Edmonds
* AGL (Attilio Giusti Leombruni)

- Anne Klein
- Aquatalia
- Bandolino
- Børn
- Christian Louboutin
- Clarks
- Cole Haan
- Ecco
- Enzo Angiolini
- Geox
- John Lobb
- Isolá
- Ivanka Trump
- Joan and David
- Jimmy Choo
- Manolo Blahnik
- Mephisto
- Me Too
- Munro
- Nine West
- Paul Green
- Rockport
- Salvatore Ferragamo
- Söfft
- Taryn Rose
- Tory Burch
- Stuart Weitzman
- Vaneli

Select a two-inch heel for stylish comfort. If you want to go higher, add a one-inch platform under the ball of the foot. A stacked or wider heel may help you feel more stable, but if a stiletto feels comfortable, listen to your feet.

Women's Fit Faux Pas

Even fashion's lost sheep will notice if you consistently set off fashion alarms. Here are some all-too-common looks to avoid at the office.

Skin Belts

When a shirt is a tad too short, or pants just a touch too low, you may flash what is known as a skin belt. It's that little sliver of skin that is exposed when either your top or your bottom—or both—doesn't fit correctly. Pair only those items that properly cover your midsection when worn together. The only belt of skin you should be showing off is the one you paid for.

Muffin Top

Muffin top mirrors the look of a fresh-baked muffin: as batter bakes, it rises and spills over the sides of the pan, creating a yummy, doughy pillow; similarly, when your pants are too tight, flesh spills over the waistband, creating a similar, but not-so-tasty, bulge. That's muffin top—a look that's delicious in the food realm, but unappetizing where fashion is concerned. Muffin top makes it look like as if you're fighting the battle of the bulge and the bulge is clearly winning.

People often tell me that the reason they have muffin top is that they just can't find pants that don't create that effect. The key is to look for pants with a higher rise; this will help contain and add structure to your midsection and prevent spillage.

Back Cleavage

Back cleavage happens when your bra band is too tight and cuts into your back, causing flesh to squeeze over the band. This faux pas is a close cousin of the double-boob, which occurs when a bra's cups are too small. In order to correct both problems, and any other bra issues you may have, treat yourself to a bra fitting. The right bra will not only help you look skinnier and make all of your tops fit better, it will ensure that your cleavage stays where it belongs—in the front of your body. Look for a lingerie boutique or specialist in your area and schedule a fitting.

VPLs (Visible Panty Lines)

Panty lines should always be invisible. Underwear is a foundation piece, meant to support your body structure in an unobtrusive way. As with the foundation of a building, one shouldn't see the undergarments supporting you beneath your clothes. Wearing underwear is like washing your hands—it's a necessary hygiene measure that should remain largely out of sight. We assume that everyone lathers up in the restroom without witnessing it for ourselves, and we should be able to assume that everyone wears underwear without the visible proof.

The best way to get rid of panty lines can be, but isn't always, a thong—as they can create visible lines, too. Seamless underwear that is sheer along the edges, or hosiery, are also good solutions. A lot of underwear is marketed as line-free, but look for something that appears as though the edges have been snipped off with a pair of scissors, allowing the underwear to lie flat against your skin with no lines. If you can't find great seamless underwear, you can also do a boy short, or a hipster style—something that isn't cut like a traditional bikini and doesn't leave a line. Just make sure they aren't too tight on your skin and don't pull across your body, creating rolls—or muffin tops.

Challenging Bust Area

If you are busty, you may have worked hard to conceal it or have become so frustrated you just let "the girls" do as they please. A little cleavage is fine, but a lot is preventable. Stay away from anything that pulls in the bust area, and always have a layering piece (cami or bandeau) underneath to help conceal and flatter. Check out collarless blazers to reduce bulk, wear V-necks instead of high necks to avoid looking top-heavy, and try monochromatic color schemes or shades of one color to elongate your figure. If you have a small bust and want to enhance your feminine figure, add long necklaces and indulge in interesting blouses. Bow tie, ruffle, and cascading-wave styles are all very flattering.

Parting Thoughts

Style is not a reward, it's a tool! Build time into your shopping experience to scout and identify the styles that work for your body type. Expect to make alterations, and schedule your budget and calendar accordingly. (I know too many people who end up leaving their alterations at the store for months because they forgot to pick them up.) Pursue the proper fit—it will always trump trends.

8

SHOP YOUR CLOSET

The first rule of my own closet is to wear what's in there. If I can't find everything easily, it means I am not using all of the pieces I own. Remember when your memory for clothes was razor-sharp and you could instantly match your new skirt to a top from two years earlier which was buried at the bottom of a drawer? Flash forward twenty years and, between family and work, most of us are lucky if we can remember a list of necessities when we go to the supermarket. I like to help "merchandise" closets so I can see everything—and I never go to the market without a list.

The parallels between clothing and food are many. If you buy fresh bread, cheese, or fruit at the farmers' market, do you try to eat it before it spoils? I'd bet your answer is yes. Yet how many times do you buy new pieces and let them hang in your closet for ages before wearing them? Of course, you might be waiting for a special occasion, trying to hunt down a matching piece, or considering if the style is too trendy for your lifestyle, but that's exactly the problem. Many people I work with open a closet full of clothes every day and say, "I have nothing to wear!" Your closet should not be a wardrobe museum, full of relics and unwearable pieces. Instead, it should be a place in your home where you go to become *you*—whether the day calls for your inner power player, mentor, multitasking working parent, or traveling salesperson. Your goal should be to make your closet a shopping destination where everything you love is in stock and fits!

Closet Consultation

If you open your closet and feel overwhelmed, then it's time to give yourself a closet consultation. If you have clothing with tags still on but are wearing the same outfits every week, then you're not making the most of your investment. Clothes, accessories, and other style furnishings are indeed an investment, of both your money and your time.

Even if you feel as though you don't have a lot of clothing in your closet, examine what's hanging in there. Do you really wear everything? Your closet is not a storage facility—each piece should have an assigned value and an expiration date.

The first step to going through your closet is to start at one end and go piece by piece, asking yourself, "Do I love it?" If possible, divide your hanging work clothes from your play clothes to make this process easier and more targeted. Prepare to make piles on your bed or around the room and to be honest with yourself. Examine each well-loved garment as if you were choosing fruits and vegetables at the market. Would you select the slightly bruised apple or the perfectly shiny one? Ideally, you should love all of your pieces; the reality is that most of us do not. We often settle because of a lack of time, funds, or even interest, just wanting to make it out of the store and back to our lives. By learning what to look for and how to shop more intelligently, you will be able to greatly reduce this inefficient use of your time. If you love or like a piece, keep it hanging in the closet. If it ranks an "okay," put it into a pile. Be realistic here. Don't tell yourself, "I spent a lot of money on it, so therefore I like it" or "It's a good brand, so I should keep it." These are not good reasons to wear something if it doesn't look good on you!

The second step is to categorize your piles. If you are not sure whether something you've selected fits, or you have owned it so long you just assume it still fits because it's a familiar number, put it in a "try-on" pile. If it doesn't fit, it goes in a "discard" pile. Clothes don't earn the right to live in your closet forever any more than they magically dress you in the morning or make their own way to a cash register. You, and only you, control these actions. Separate items that are too big from those that are too small, as well as items that need slight alterations (hem or sleeves are too long, missing button, small hole or tear).

Style Alert: *Clothes don't always look better just because they cost more or because you scored a deal on a prestige brand.*

I also want you to examine garments for stains and tears. If the damage is fixable, place the item in the alterations pile; if not, let it go. The "let it go" pile will probably be one of the bigger ones. We often have a tough time letting go of favorite items that are stained, but if you have tried to remove the stain to no avail, then keeping it in the business category is not an option. Pit stains and ring around the collar count, too. Your closet should not be the place stained clothes go to die.

The third step is to look inside your closet and assess whether it's stocked with items that match your lifestyle. Do you have a career in sales but a closet full of cardigans? Maybe you need to invest in additional power pieces. Are you a recent grad dressing as if you were still in college? Fast-fashion stores like H&M, Zara, The Limited, Express, and capsule collections at JCPenney, Kohl's, and Target make it easy and affordable to shop for work clothes on a budget. Or did you recently change jobs so you now have clothing that works only in a different industry or for a different dress code? Dressing appropriately for the lifestyle you are living helps foster and maintain confidence. There are enough distractions in life without your closet being one of them. Streamline your shopping decisions and set the bar high. Only pieces that you love, that fit well, and that work for your lifestyle should make it home to your closet.

One category of unnecessary items people often have in their closets are what I call ghosts. These are friends from yesteryear, highlighting important occasions from your past: the suit you wore to your law-school graduation, your father's corduroy blazer, your engagement-party ensemble (that you hope will work one day on a resort-casual trip), or one of my favorites—an item from the store Country Road, which closed in the United States over ten years ago! If you have the room to allow your closet to be a wardrobe museum, exhibiting all past purchases and memories, terrific. Most people don't.

When saving items, do so for a good reason and limit the number. For example, Jim had an excessive number of baseball hats. His job was baseball related, and though he never wore any of the hats, he loved having them as mementos. Eventually, they overran his closet and he barely had room for the important stuff like shoes, sweaters, and casual wear—all available shelving went to hats. When I arrived to help organize his space, we discussed his attachment to these hats, and he realized that, while he loved them, he felt overwhelmed and stifled by his collection. To maximize his physical (and emotional) space, I created a decorative wall in his closet so he could admire his top-twenty baseball caps; the rest were put away in a box in the basement. He was free to rotate his featured twenty hats, but now they added decorative value instead of just taking up space. This freedom made it easier for him to let go—often one of the hardest things for us to do in our closets. In fact, the biggest obstacle to embracing a new style resides in the mind.

Hanging alongside the ghosts in our closets are those pieces that might come back into style or fit again. While fashions do come back, bodies sometimes don't. Try not to hang onto something for longer than three years without wearing it unless it has a very specific purpose. I know a few savvy women who love to shop at work-staple destinations like Ann Taylor, Banana Republic, J.Crew, and Talbots but hate that everyone else in their office is also shopping there. They will actually buy and save star pieces for a couple of years and wear them only after everyone else has cycled through them, so that no one will remember these once hung on every mannequin in the city. This takes a well-honed eye and a bit of planning, but if you have the space and budget to house items, give it a try. This is one of the only times I allow clients to keep pieces with tags.

I also know women who save their money and buy amazing designer pieces—a pair of Manolo Blahniks, a Chanel handbag, a Diane von Furstenberg wrap dress, a David Yurman necklace—and save them forever. In fact, five years after the purchase date, such items might very well be sitting in their original packaging. This is not productive "saving." Your money would be better off sitting in a retirement account. If you are a member of the "buy and hold" club, march over to that fabulous piece and ask yourself why you're not wearing it. Do you think you don't deserve it? Doesn't it fit your lifestyle? Is it too much for the office? Usually, these pieces are classics and an amazing opportunity but we might be trigger-shy or waiting for the perfect moment...one that may never come.

Everything in your closet should be wearable. Create moments to interact with your clothing and accessories—otherwise, they become dollar bills on hangers. If you've made a big-ticket purchase only to find later that it wasn't the right match, try consigning the item to recoup some of your cost and then move on. Over time, amazing pieces must be edited out of your wardrobe simply because a style has expired— yes, sometimes before you're able to debut them.

Once your piles are created, the next step is assessment. At this point, you should have at least three piles: one for items to try on, one for items that need action (alterations, stain removal), and one for give-aways. Of course, you can further divide these according to specific details. In the "action items," divide pieces that can be easily altered from those that are too small or way too big. Separate those pieces that need to go to the dry cleaner from ones you can treat at home. And, in the giveaway group, decide which pieces go to people you know and which are destined for charitable organizations. It feels good to donate items, whether sharing clothes with your nanny, a thrift-store patron, or a stranger learning to dress to impress with the help of a charitable organization. Don't save your clothes for a "right time" donation, or they'll stay in your guest-room closet longer than they did in yours.

Style Alert: *If you are hesitant to give away clothes, organize a swap party with friends or consider selling designer duds on eBay. One person's unwanted piece could be another's treasure!*

Closet Organization: What's Left Hanging?

Now that you've made your piles, your closet should be filled with the items you need and love. Take a look inside: Is there much in there? I'm betting most of what's hanging up is what you actually wear or wish you wore to work, and that what's on the bed is excess or nostalgic items you would only get rid of if forced. Consider this your motivation. Remove the empty hangers from your closet. Assess the amount of space you now have and revel in it. We tend to wear 20 percent of our wardrobe 80 percent of the time. Most of the time, when I clean out a closet, clients are pleasantly surprised to note that the process of rebuilding their wardrobes is neither as painful nor as expensive as they expected. We rarely get rid of brand-new pieces that are stylish—we let go of stained, dated, ill-fitting garments that have not been worn in years but take up a lot of space.

A well-edited closet provides you with the opportunity to clearly identify the gaps in your wardrobe and shop your closet to create new combinations. The first step is to visually organize your newly revised space so that these opportunities are clearly visible. Once you remove the extras, try to hang everything on the same kind of hanger—whether these are wire hangers from the dry cleaner or elegant wooden ones. Hangers in different styles and colors are distracting to the eye, especially when laden with clothing, so do your best to create a streamlined, elegant look by only using one style. Think of your favorite places to shop—is it easier to find that perfect piece at a well-organized boutique or on the overcrowded racks at your local discounter? But be mindful of the amount of time you have for this project. If it's too overwhelming, it could be left untouched or half-finished.

This "merchandizing" process is about the action of organizing your space and making it as attractive and easy to shop as your favorite boutique. If you are looking for a hanger recommendation, one of my favorite styles is the slim and velvet collection available at a variety of retailers, including QVC, HSN, Target, The Container Store, Costco, and Bed Bath & Beyond. This type of hanger works especially well if you are tight on space, and will help prevent your clothing from slipping off the hanger. Plan for at least half an inch of space between hangers (more if your hangers are thicker) so you can comfortably move them as you browse your closet. If you do not have enough hangers at home, add them to your shopping list as you identify the gaps in your wardrobe.

The next step is to choose a method of visual organization that works for you. Some people like to organize by color (light to dark) or category (suits, pants, skirts). For women, my favorite method is to start by sleeve length—line up your shirts starting from sleeveless to long-sleeve and, if so inclined, organize by color within each category. Move on to third pieces and dresses, also organizing by sleeve length. If you've ever wondered what colors look best on you, look in your closet, because chances are you already own them. As you organize tops, third pieces, and dresses, you will understand how color plays a role in your wardrobe—do you stock up on neutrals or buy only brights? You don't need to own every color in the rainbow, just the ones that are flattering.

Once you reach pants and skirts, organize shortest to longest and again by color if you so desire. If you have enough long hanging space in your closet, hang pants using clip hangers to save space instead of folding them over a hanger. Next comes the matter of positioning these items—here, it's best to merchandise the items that are most challenging to wear and those that get frequent use in a well-lit, prominent place. For example, if you decide what to wear every day by the way your stomach feels (bloated or skinny), you may want to have your pants easily accessible so you can try them on in the morning. If you wear a third piece daily, showcase third pieces in the center instead of using that valuable space for layering tops and shells. When you organize items by sleeve length and hem, you will clearly see what you own. Then merchandise by spotlighting the categories you wear the most or wish you wore more often.

Men can also follow a similar method of organization. Categories for your work essentials may be more limited, but identify them anyway. Divide shirts by arranging them from casual to formal, by sleeve length and color. Separate pants from suits, and isolate sport coats. If you have trouble pairing ties with shirts, consider making combinations in advance and hanging them together. You are more likely to wear accessories (cuff links, brass collar stays, tie clips) if you can find them, so keep them nearby.

Through this process you will begin to discover multiples of the same item, pieces with tags, and forgotten or incomplete outfits. Our tendency is to buy multiple versions of the same item repeatedly until we get it right. Many times this happens with a "risky" fashion item, when we're trying out a new color or style. Ladies, remember when you wanted to try that tunic for a particular ensemble? Perhaps the first time you rushed to buy it you were on your lunch break and spotted an unbeatable sale price. You wore it once and realized it didn't work. Later, you bought another version of a tunic, and now you love it! This happens to men, too—you take a risk on a lavender shirt and don't like it but keep the shirt anyway. Father's Day comes around and with it another lavender shirt, but this time it's perfect! Often, we forget to give away or trade out the versions that don't work. There was never really anything wrong with it; you simply found something you liked better. Make this an actionable item: every time you replace a style get rid of the old one (donate or swap) or move it to a different category (from work to play). This will help prevent a growing number of excess items in your wardrobe.

Where to Put Your Accessories

Once your clothes have been merchandised, move on to your accessories. Shoes are a prominent category. Remove the pairs you wear most from boxes or even those clear storage containers. (Save these for seasonal storage.) Face them toward you, or arrange them so one shoe is facing forward and the other heel forward, for a better sense of the look and to see when they start to get scuffed or appear old. Keep an eye on the heels, but understand that most people notice the front of your shoes first. Ladies, display pashminas in your closet so they are easy to add to an outfit, and keep handbags outside of their dust covers if you like to change them frequently. When we store items, we are less likely to wear them because they can't be found at a moment's notice.

Create a jewelry boutique—either in a well-organized drawer or atop a dresser. Hang necklaces and bracelets on a jewelry tree for easy access. Men, hang ties near dress shirts so combinations can easily be made, and store belts where you'll notice wear or overuse. It's important to hang as much as your space permits, keeping just the basics folded. Items in drawers or on shelves are often forgotten, so limit them to casual wear, layering pieces, and furnishings.

Managing Your Clothes

How do you know if you have too much? Every time I walk into a closet, I get questions about the smallest or biggest, most organized or disorganized closet I have ever seen and how my current client compares. The trick to knowing whether you own the right amount of clothing is noting if you have enough time in your schedule to wear it all. In any given closet, you need only fourteen to twenty-two pieces a season (not including accessories) for a successful and stylish work wardrobe. Gasp, I know! But less is truly more. And some pieces will overlap during a season change. Think back to the 20 percent of your wardrobe that you actually wear. Go count how many pieces of clothing that encompasses. While a style maven will happily double or triple that number, the reality is you should own and cultivate only the collection you can actually wear. Just as with food, portion control is important and everyone has a different tolerance.

Gabby loves shopping so much that barely a day goes by that she doesn't come home with something new. Whether it's on her lunch break or while traveling for work and hitting major shopping destinations between meetings, she packs her closet with fabulous items. And Gabby not only loves shopping, she has great taste, too! The challenge for her is that she doesn't have time to pull together or coordinate outfits. She only enjoys the shopping experience. Similarly, Ted is a bargain shopper and loves to chase sales. It is almost impossible to stop him. He often buys clothes he has absolutely no need for because the thrill of the hunt and the bargain-basement price tags excite him. If you fall on either side of this spectrum, you share a common trait: you are buying more items—either "of the moment" trends or replenishment basics on sale—than you have days to wear them. If you find yourself permanently storing clothes (not counting off-season items) in more than three closets around your house, or in the attic, garage, or basement, then you have too much stuff. The only people who should have that much are the ones who can't be seen shopping in public because of paparazzi or security issues. The average person needs a shoppable closet, not an entire department store. The size of your kitchen pantry is a good analogy for a closet—keep only as much food as you can eat, and only as much clothing as you can wear.

Seasonal Dressing

Depending where you live, your clothing may heavily favor one season or cover all four. Except in extreme climates, most wardrobes work well in three seasons. In terms of organization, make sure to circulate clothing for relevant seasons. If you have the luxury of another closet, go ahead and move things that you won't be wearing once the weather cools or heats up. Just like your favorite stores, feature wearable clothes as often as you can. There is no need to sort through tweeds in the summer or linen in the winter. If you don't have additional space, put the fabrics and colors for a different season at the back of the closet. This same advice applies for those storing various sizes of transitional clothing, either due to pregnancy, or a shift in weight in their everyday closet.

Style Alert: *Items you buy in the spring often still work in the fall. Consider layering items throughout the year to get more bang for your buck.*

The Sizes in Your Closet

Many men and women fluctuate waist size in any given week by three to five pounds. For some, this means a size change (moving up or down); for others it's a style adjustment (not wearing a particular type of garment until the proper weight returns). It is completely rational to have clothes that will accommodate your body as it fluctuates. However, using clothing of the wrong size in order to inspire yourself is not a good idea. Keeping items that are too small can be damaging to your self-esteem, and storing items three sizes too big (because you are scared you will become that size again) is not an effective use of space (physically or mentally).

When I first walked into Eddy's closet, I was struck by how many labels he had posted around his space. At first glance, I thought this might be an ingrained solution for a habitual label maker to identify his clothes, but as I got up close, I saw these were old pieces of paper with words such as "fat" and "skinny"—and he wasn't talking about skinny jeans! I asked him what all the labels meant and he explained that they identified danger zones—places he didn't want to visit in his closet. "Fat" directed the eye to pants from when he was fat (seven years earlier) and "skinny" were for shirts from when he was skinnier (four years earlier). He had maintained the same body shape and weight for the last three years but he had kept his old clothes as reminders. He also had a damaged goods section—items labeled too short or too long, stained, or ripped. Eddy's closet was a war zone; almost anything he touched could bring up a negative memory or feeling.

A well-organized closet is not always a shoppable one. The key to shoppability is maintaining a well-edited wardrobe. The methods we use to organize and store our clothing can either help or hinder our development. Style and clothing are tools to help you manage your weight—not rewards for losing it. We have been conditioned to think, "I'll go shopping when I lose twenty pounds" instead of going shopping when we lose five so that we look and feel great—thus motivated to maintain or continue to shed the pounds.

Styling a life change is a long-term process. When a person makes the decision to lose a significant amount of weight (twenty-five to one hundred pounds), new clothes are a necessity and I work with clients monthly to help them manage their wardrobes as they drop sizes. This type of transition cannot be hidden behind baggy clothes or closed doors. My clients go to work every day, climbing the ladder of success.

Depending on the pattern of weight loss, the move between sizes can occur every five to ten pounds. The trick to managing this process without going into debt is to remember that less is more and that looking good in a transition period doesn't require the most expensive pieces. Still, you may be on a promotion track or interviewing while losing weight, and it's important to keep your look current. The most rewarding part of this journey is watching people get to show off their hard work every step of the way.

I worked with Roberta during a critical professional juncture in her life. She was a rising star in the media world and on a quest to lose seventy-five pounds. While she was excited to shed the weight, she didn't want every conversation in her professional life to focus on her body. We decided to update her wardrobe every time her size changed, about every four weeks, to keep her look seamless and modern. Losing a significant amount of weight is a long journey; your stops along the way should feel good and get you accustomed to your size. While dramatically changing size is rewarding, it can also be an emotional rollercoaster.

When we first started, Roberta didn't really notice when her pants were too big—she just thought they were becoming comfortable. Trying on and wearing clothes in your appropriate size is often an issue of mental and emotional acceptance rather than a matter of physical ease. By the fourth time we bought new pants for Roberta, she could finally feel which ones were too big, and she began to associate that feeling with a need to change sizes. People who have lost a great deal of weight often see themselves in the mirror as bigger than they really are. It's important to take baby steps and nurture the weight-loss process. By taking stock of her new body every month, Roberta got used to the feeling of clothing starting out a little tighter, stretching out, being washed and shrinking, then feeling larger as she lost weight. It also forced her to look in the mirror. Roberta became an expert at navigating these sensitive waters and started to revel in the woman she was becoming.

Stocking Your Closet with Work Essentials

You can't build an ideal wardrobe without the proper foundation. Work essentials for both men and women are available at every price point and will help you climb the ladder of success. If you don't already have them, stock up on these classic items, which you can restyle with accessories, and start getting more bang for your buck. (Remember, accessories take up less closet space than clothing!) These are foundation pieces that will help build (or update) your professional wardrobe. They're dress-code-appropriate, can be worn in a variety of ways, and can be styled with trendier accessories for a fresh look.

WARDROBE ESSENTIALS

Essentials for Women at Work

- Black pants: Fitted through the backside and hips but not skin tight, this is the workhorse of any work wardrobe.
- Pencil skirt: This knee-length fitted skirt is both classic and modern. Sleek and ultra-feminine, it adds style power to any wardrobe. Choose black or a neutral color for the utmost versatility.
- White Oxford shirt or white third piece: Whether a fitted version with French cuffs or an oversized style cinched with a belt, this staple will always be an office classic. If the buttons pull, it doesn't fit! Opt for a stylish white blazer for a fresh take on a timeless look.
- Blazer: This key third piece can be worn with pants or skirts, or belted with a dress. Look for a slim fit in the shoulders and an easy-to-spot waist—stay away from excess material for a clean, professional look.

- Cardigan: A comfortable, expensive-looking cardigan will always be business casual–friendly.
- Trouser jeans: Denim in a dark, clean wash is stylish and works on casual Fridays, or for more laid-back office environments.
- Little black dress: This ultimate day-to-night piece should be the first thing you reach for when you have a function right after work. Add statement jewelry, a wrap, or heels to instantly transition this dress to cocktail hour.
- An everyday work dress: An everyday dress is a go-to piece for the modern woman. Layer a third piece over a sleeveless sheath, show off your shape in a wrap-style dress, or select a classic shirt-dress for the office.
- Trench coat: It's timeless, flattering, and works across the seasons. An added bonus is its connection to the golden age of Hollywood's glamorous leading ladies.
- Wrap: Toss a cozy pashmina or ruffled, wool wrap over your shoulders for instant glamour and warmth.
- Belt: A medium to wide style in elastic with a patent leather buckle will highlight your waist and keep you comfortable all day. A leather obi belt (a leather sash) is another personal favorite of mine.
- Shoes: Closed-toe black patent heels or pointy flats are classic, versatile, and sophisticated. Nude heels are essential in the warmer months to elongate your legs—match your skin tone and opt for a closed-toe or peep-toe style.
- Shapewear: Stand straighter, shape the hips, and tuck in the tummy with shapewear. Maintain a collection that works year-round with dresses, skirts, or pants.
- Sunglasses: Everyone needs a great pair of shades to hide behind during a lunch break or daily commute.
- Statement jewelry: A long silver or gold necklace (between thirty and thirty-two inches in length) is almost always slimming; it draws attention to your upper torso and bust.
- Nail polish: Keep a stash of classic faves like ballet-slipper pink, soft white, and boardroom-standout red.

(Continued)

- Tote or briefcase: Often guarding a laptop, files, and makeup, your bag does a lot of talking for you, so invest wisely. A stiff leather tote that looks neat could be Goyard or even a special collection for Target.

Essentials for Men at Work

- Flat-front slacks: Modern and professional, these pants seamlessly float from business formal to business casual.
- Suiting: Invest in a well-tailored navy or gray single-breasted suit. Save black for formal occasions.
- Versatile blazer: Choose a navy blazer or patterned sport coat to take you from day to night.
- Dress shirts: Versatile from business casual to formal, find the right fit for your physique and invest in a variety of colors. Iron-free styles offer easy at-home maintenance.
- Dark jeans: Tailored, conservative styles are acceptable at many offices on casual days. Look for modern bootcut or straight-leg denim in a dark wash.
- Wrinkle-free khakis: Keep this business-casual classic professional with a well-tailored, clean look.
- Nice shoes: People do look down, so invest in at least one pair of high-quality shoes. Remember that they'll get a lot of wear and be sure to match your dress code. Look for loafers or lace-ups with a slim, almond-shaped toe.
- Furnishings: Look for socks that match the color of your pants or bright patterns to add a unique flair, belts to match the exact color of your shoes (not just the same color family), and undershirts to prevent others from seeing chest hair, tattoos, or perspiration.
- Accessories: Add brass collar stays to help your dress collar shirts look neater, carry a nice wallet or money clip for the unexpected trip to the coffee shop with your boss, and wear a nice, sleek watch that matches your overall look (could be an everyday Timex or a more expensive Rolex).
- Coat: Select outerwear appropriate to your locale and dress code—then make sure it has a tailored and modern look.

After you've accumulated these basics, you can really begin to "shop your closet" and transform your space into your own favorite shopping destination. How can a crowded, messy, picked-over store filled with items in every imaginable shape, size, and style compete with a collection of clothing that fits and flatters you perfectly? Shopping your closet saves time, aggravation, and, most importantly, money. You'll no longer buy unnecessary or unsuitable items, and you'll learn to look great with items you already own—the key to dressing well on a budget.

Guidelines for Keeping your Clothes Clean

Now that you've created a shoppable closet, it is important to maintain your duds in mint condition. Be mindful and hang up clothes that can be worn again before they go to the dry cleaner. Pants can usually get three to five wears before starting to lose their shape; shirts crease much more quickly. Suiting and blazers can often go six weeks to six months before they need a cleaning, unless they have a stain or an odor. Be sure to clean all pieces of your suit together so they wear evenly. When washing clothes at home, pretreat stains in a timely manner and use Woolite Darks on black clothing and darker items to help maintain their color. When shoes beg for a polishing beyond your at-home ritual or need a sole replacement, take them to the cobbler to be refreshed.

Style Alert: *To save on dry cleaning costs, take care of your machine-washable wardrobe at home and only bring it to the dry cleaners to be pressed for a crisp look.*

There will come a time when you'll have to decide to stop wearing a garment to the office. Learn to spot the signs a piece should be removed from public view: fading; permanent stains or overall dinginess; nubby or pilly surfaces; rips, tears, and fraying that cannot be fixed. If an item is truly damaged, consider retiring it from "at home" use as well—it may need to go to the wardrobe graveyard, where all once-great fashion goes in the end.

Parting Thoughts

You will discover your unique style DNA as you shop your closet. Each season, manage your wardrobe and take note of gaps that need to be filled. Stock your closet with a customized selection of clothing that is age-appropriate, on-trend, fits well, and is reflective of your lifestyle, and you will build a wardrobe that stands the test of time. As your signature style begins to emerge, it will become easier to get dressed and walk out the door feeling confident!

9
SHOPPING WITHOUT AN EXPENSE ACCOUNT

LAUREN'S LUST LIST
- Elbow-length black leather gloves
- Metallic clutch (with hidden strap)
- Platform suede heels

* ongoing items: third pieces, dark jeans, pointy-toe flats, statement necklaces

I never go shopping without a list. It's dangerous! I might overspend my budget (or my client's) or buy things I don't need. At any given time, I have an entry on my phone named "lust list." Here, I keep items I am lusting after as well as basics I should always keep an eye out for, should I find myself with an extra hour, or three, on a lucky day.

You know when you're getting dressed and just wish you had the perfect something to complete your outfit? When that happens to me, it goes on my lust list immediately! Every time I work with a client, I conclude our closet appointment with a shopping list that includes items to fill noticeable wardrobe gaps. This will keep us targeted and on track, as well as give my client a sense of what to expect when we hit the stores.

It's particularly important to be strategic when it comes to shopping. It's so easy to feel lost and overwhelmed when you shop. If you don't like shopping, checking items off a list will help you stay on task and offer a feeling of accomplishment for an otherwise stressful activity. If you love shopping but already have everything, a lust list is a great way to pinpoint allowable indulgences when you find yourself speeding through your favorite sport. How many times have you bought more of something you love instead of pieces you need?

Men are often replenishment shoppers; many women find the act of shopping a soothing activity. Men are more likely to buy full-price items; women are more likely to enjoy chasing down bargains (and later recounting their adventures). Full price, however, can sometimes mean a pair of $29 Dockers, and a bargain for some can be defined as a pair of designer shoes at Saks Fifth Avenue Off Fifth for $300. Sale racks can be enticing and are often a person's first stop when entering a store. Beware, though: they are best left to the seasoned shopper with time to pick over what's offered. With a list in hand, you are sure to navigate the racks with ease and confidence.

Stretching Your Dollar

You can create a stylish wardrobe on any budget. Most of us do not have endless money for clothes and accessories, and while I know a few folks who may eat Ramen for a week just to afford a fabulous piece, many of us need to keep our budgets and bellies in check. My first piece of advice: spend the most time (and sometimes dollars) on the hardest part of your body to fit. For women, that usually means searching for the perfect fit on the hips, midsection, or bust; for men, it means getting the length right on a pair of pants or achieving the best fit through the torso.

Similarly, spend the most money on pieces you wear the most. There can be regional differences here as well. Everyday slacks and a stylish third piece or sport coat might work best for the director of a nonprofit; a trench coat and tote are better investments for the city-commuting consultant who jumps on the subway daily. It is important to shop for the lifestyle you lead. Often, the treasured pieces I find in my clients' closets hardly get face time: a pair of heels too high to walk in, a designer skirt that never coordinated with a top, or a fancy dress shirt that feels too loud for work.

Quality is not as important as fit. A piece that is well-tailored (or one you are lucky enough to have fit you off the rack) can trump an ill-fitting, high-quality piece. Fast fashion is so normal in our culture that people are shopping for work basics in the same stores they buy paper towels in bulk. An attendee at one of my style seminars told me her husband had ordered two new sport coats, six dress shirts, and three pairs of dress pants at Costco. And she wasn't embarrassed to admit it. Even five years ago, shopping at Kohl's, JCPenney, or Sears—let alone Costco—was hardly the badge of honor it is today. The presence of design giants like Vera Wang, Joseph Aboud, and even the Kardashians at a variety of discount retailers has completely shifted the way we shop. So be grateful for bargains, and expect to pay for alterations when shopping off the rack. A good tailor on speed dial is essential.

The Difference Between Buying Cheap and Looking Cheap

It has long been a fashionista's secret to mix high and low fashions. No public figure has brought this concept to center stage more than First Lady Michelle Obama. She appears equally comfortable dressed in casual threads from the Gap or a Jason Wu gown. She even made history on Inauguration Day in 2009 by combining everyday basics from J.Crew with Isabel Toledo haute couture. Her faithful audience takes note and follows in her footsteps.

The difference between buying items that are inexpensive and looking cheap lies in two things: fit and fabric. If they're good, you're good, no matter where you're shopping. Whether you choose to dress high end one day and low end another, or combine high and low items in the same look, you want to keep your overall style consistent. If you dress like a superstar during the week but in rags on the weekend, it doesn't count. Don't violate the spirit of your great workaday fashion by dressing like a slob in your downtime. (I know people who do this!) However, if you always look polished and professional, people will assume you invest in your appearance.

Textured items do really well in the cheap-chic category, as do accessories. Look for embellished pieces, prints, shoes, jewelry, and wraps. For example, pair a classic black sheath with a stylish third piece, such as a statement necklace, and funky designer shoes from a well-known designer's capsule collection at Payless. A handbag, on the other hand, can immediately look cheap. If exotic leathers are beyond your budget (or against your principles), look for a similarly textured fabric in simulated ostrich or embossed snakeskin, or a style in linen, tweed, or cotton.

Many designers include jewelry in their collections, which is always fun to add to an outfit. If your overall ensemble reads neat, stylish, and well-fitting, then costume jewelry will look playful instead of cheap. Basics and standout trend items at cheap-chic retailers like Zara, H&M, and Topshop are also great to include in your wardrobe. You can often find good pieces for layering, as well as a few workhorses for your wardrobe. They may not last as long (though they might if you take good care of them), but depending on your goals, they could work and blend well into a high–low style of dress. Carry a designer bag, wear Payless heels and a well-tailored black suit from Zara, and no one will be the wiser!

Sometimes, it's just cool to brag about wearing something inexpensive. Special designer capsule collections, like Karl Lagerfeld's at H&M in 2004, or those by any of the designers who have been part of the Go International brand at Target, like Missoni in 2011, always attract such attention. And not only is it hip to wear such pieces and brag about it, they can sometimes be found on eBay selling for double the original price! A great bargain at high-end outlets is also a terrific, braggable find. Barneys, Brioni, Armani, Ferragamo, St. John, Tom Ford, Rag & Bone, Gucci, Prada, Valentino, Neiman Marcus, and Saks Fifth Avenue are among the luxury retailers with outlet locations. Keep your lust list handy so you don't feel like a kid in the candy store next time you find yourself in shopping heaven!

Style Alert: *High-end outlet shopping is definitely worth the trip for a bargain-hunting fashionista! Catching the bus directly from JFK or the Port Authority to Woodbury Commons in Central Valley, New York, is a pilgrimage for those in the know.*

When to Save, Spend, and Splurge

Trends have a way of turning into timeless classics; fads are a flash in the pan. For example, the pointy-toe pump will forever be in the fabric of a stylish woman's career wardrobe. It goes through its evolutions— stacked heel to stiletto, rounded point to roach-killer—but it will never completely disappear. Fads like neons, embellished shirt collars, and faux glasses, on the other hand, are in style (and available) only for a season or two. An item or style becomes a trend after at least three to five years on shelves, and a fad is a cool movement that can last for up to a year. Some fads can be fabulous, while there are a few trends I wish would just disappear. The question to ask yourself when shopping is, "Do these trends (or fads) work for my body type, age, and budget?"

Skinny jeans began as a fad that morphed into a trend once the skinny black pant became an office staple. Depending on your height and overall look, skinnies can be worn with high heels or flats, but they are actually a difficult style to master. Most skinny pants cannot be treated like traditional cuts. Shirts need to be longer and their length proportionate to body type.

When Rhonda showed up wearing skinny pants to work almost daily, her company's Human Resources department called me in to intervene. Rhonda was tucking her shirts in, revealing unsightly bulges in the crotch area and showing off a tightly fitted backside and thigh. Her coworkers were justifiably uncomfortable with her unprofessional dress, and several had complained to management.

There are far worse versions of this style story. Everyone I've interviewed who's been called out on this fashion citation answers the same way: "I wear these pants because they are the only style I see when I go shopping!" Skinnies can add about five pounds to your overall look, and I advise wearing them only if you can afford the extra weight. If you work in a casual environment, pair them with long tops or jackets and knee-high boots or flats, to draw the eye downward, balancing the tight fit above. They work best on straight body types; confident, skinny curvies and pears who like to show off their hips; and apples who wear them only with tunics. Everyone else, beware! Keep searching the racks for styles that work for you. Often, women who aren't even trying to become trend followers get pulled into the current of a forceful fashion trend.

But, fear not! Sometimes, a fabulous trend does come along. Black and white (as solids, prints, polka dots, or stripes) can be easily shopped in your own closet and is flattering on almost everyone. A trend like this is splurge-worthy, whereas skinnies aren't unless it's the right fit for your body type. Keep an eye on the trends of the season until you spot the perfect style and color for you. When a trend catches on, enjoy the fringe benefit of watching it blossom at every price point.

Expect to shop at least once a season (every three months) and spend enough to update your wardrobe with three to seven new pieces. Interns might spend $200 and CEOs $2000. Factor in a little more into your budget if it's time to add a wow piece or you're starting to build your wardrobe from scratch.

Style Alert: *Be thrifty. Bring along coupons or ask at the register for any special discounts or incentives currently being offered. Often times, being a teacher, member of the military, or AAA member will yield ten percent off your purchase—all you have to do is ask.*

WHEN TO SAVE, SPEND, AND SPLURGE

Save:

- On pieces that fit you easily from less expensive manufacturers
- On overly trendy or fad items with an expiration date

(Continued)

- On colorful additions to your wardrobe
- *Women, save on:* layering pieces (like shells), costume jewelry, a trench or raincoat, and shoes
- *Men, save on:* accessories, ties, socks, and coats

Spend:

- On items for hard-to-fit areas on your physique
- On the workhorses of your wardrobe
- On good-quality items your audience sees daily
- *Women, spend on*: black pants, dark denim, third pieces, shape-wear, hair care, skin care, and makeup
- *Men, spend on*: suiting, properly tailored pants, dress shirts, grooming, and skin care

Splurge:

- When you find the perfect fit and it cannot be replicated
- When your wardrobe needs a wow piece to complement everyday workhorses
- When you've earned it
- *Women, splurge on*: designer handbags, designer shoes, jewelry, suiting, and third pieces
- *Men, splurge on*: computer case or briefcase, shoes, dressier denim for versatility, custom clothing

It's Time to go Shopping!

You've cleaned out your closet and identified the gaps in your wardrobe. You've learned guidelines on fit and strategies for when to splurge and when to save. Now it's time to shop! Treat your trip like a doctor's appointment and come prepared. Do your pre-work, identifying the right spots to shop (mall or boutique district), bringing along images you may have found online or in magazines to inspire you. If necessary, break up your list and give yourself specific goals like, "Today, I am shopping for two third pieces" or "I need one suit and a dress shirt."

Give yourself two to three uninterrupted hours. Leave the kids at home and your phone on vibrate. Don't come hungry. Carry an energy bar or other energy-rich snack and water, in case the air in the fitting room is dry (which is often the case in malls). Don't suck in your stomach or stand on your toes every time you look in the mirror. Do what you can to control the situation so you feel good when you look in the mirror—bring appropriate shoes and shapewear to make your shopping experience as realistic as possible. If heels make you feel skinny or flats are the only sole comfort that work, have them on hand or plan to buy new ones.

Map and shopping list in hand, identify the right stores or departments within stores. Start with scouting items off your list, and when you find one, grab it in two sizes—the size you hope you are and the size you might be. How many times have you tried something on in the fitting room and needed the next size? There isn't a salesperson in sight and you begin to get frustrated. This can easily lead to abandonment of the shopping session. Be proactive and grab two, or even three, sizes to make it convenient for yourself.

Start trying things on and actually look in the mirror. Keep clothes on long enough to analyze your look and identify what you do and don't like. Keep in mind that clothes need stretching and that not all sizes are created equal. If you are in between sizes on a particular item, try on several in the same size and give it a good whirl before deciding if it's too small. I know that if I'm not in the dressing room with clients, they often remove a garment before fully zipping it because it feels too tight. Sometimes, I feel like a personal trainer with the exercises I help guide clients through to stretch out a pair of pants! We do a variety of squats and stretches before deciding whether an item is too tight. This is a great shortcut for both men and women that mimics life's movements and usually stretches out clothes. If a piece still doesn't feel right, look in the mirror and use this item to help you select better ones. If you start doing a happy dance, then you know you've struck gold with a look you'll probably be excited to wear to work the following day.

As you shop at different stores, don't be afraid to put things on hold. It can be helpful to get perspective; have a coffee, call a friend, run an errand in the mall, and then come back. If you need another opinion, ask a fellow shopper or salesperson, or take a picture of yourself with your phone and e-mail it to a loved one. But in the long run, it's better to try to make as many decisions as possible in the store and avoid feverish returning—an exhausting and costly activity.

Try to buy complete outfits instead of lone pieces that will wait in your closet for a companion. Look in your closet to see how many items have suffered. Are there ones that still hang with tags, never worn because you didn't know how to match them? Assign strategic value to your clothes; know where and when you will wear them to make the most out of your investment and ensure they don't sit in your closet collecting dust. Unless an item is for a special occasion, if you haven't worn it within two weeks of purchase, return it or force yourself to give it a try. If you're buying in high volume, take pictures of your combinations in the fitting room to make them easier to remember at home.

Shopping with an Expert

If the thought of shopping alone sends you reaching for Xanax, consider outsourcing this activity, hiring an expert for help, or bringing along a friend or relative. Your time is valuable, and if you're short on this commodity, you may want to work with a personal shopper, stylist, or wardrobe or image consultant. This is also an excellent investment for the person looking for individualized advice and wardrobe planning. These four job descriptions are invariably linked, and depending on the city where you live, the semantics may differ.

At one time, a personal shopper was limited to shopping in only one store, typically as a department store employee. The term "stylist" was borrowed from Hollywood and initially meant someone who worked with celebrities, on movie sets, the red carpet, or magazine shoots. A wardrobe consultant is someone who will help you both at your home and in stores—the evolution of a personal shopper. An image consultant shares much of a wardrobe consultant's job description, but also examines your overall executive presence and color palette to help prepare a personalized style scheme for you. These titles are, or should be, based on the background and career of the expert.

More and more non-celebs are seeking style assistance these days, and the industry has exploded with "experts" working both at stores and independently. My best advice: choose your expert the way you would choose a therapist. This will be someone who will probably see you naked—both inside and out. You'll be forming a bond with this person, so make sure he or she truly understands your goals. Find out if consultants work on commission, and try to get a referral from an existing client. Keep in mind that those just starting out will charge less, but industry veterans have greater experience (and with more body types). Don't be intimidated by a "younger" or "hipper" fashion professional. You don't need someone who dresses like you; you want a confident person who understands your mind-set and shape.

If hiring an expert falls outside your budget, work with an in-store personal shopper (this service is free and does not require a minimum purchase) or a talented salesperson, or bring along a friend, family member, or even a coworker. But bear in mind that there is a difference between shopping with someone else and bringing someone along whose presence will be helpful. If you are insecure, don't bring someone skinnier or with a bigger budget who's shopping in the same category as you (e.g., you both need pants for work). Try to bring someone who is supportive instead of judgmental, is fun to hang out with, and will give you honest feedback. In fact, the same advice applies if you hire an expert!

Everyday Shopping Strategies

To:	LaurenLovesToShop
From:	Piperlime@piperlime.com
Subject:	20% Sitewide!

Everyone loves a sale, but it's important to know which ones are worth shopping. Stores have so many incentives, you'll be told you're getting a bargain almost daily.

First step, sign up for coupons from your favorite stores. I have mine sent to a dedicated, free e-mail account so they don't clog up my personal e-mail. Second, see if there are any additional incentives for interacting with the store via text, social media, or apps on your phone. Often "liking" a company on Facebook or entering a contest on Twitter can yield a discount well worth the trouble. Third, sign up for newsletters offered by your favorite retailers so you can stay up to date on sales and promotions.

Style Alert: *Be a savvy shopper, always on the lookout for your favorite items to go on sale. If you made a full-price purchase and spot your item on sale soon thereafter, bring in the receipt and many retailers will give you a price adjustment. Similarly, many big box retailers will match their competitor's price when shown that competitor's advertisement.*

My favorite type of sale is "Friends and Family." It happens twice a year at many department stores and a few select boutiques and chain stores. The lovely part of these events is a typical discount of 20 percent off both full-price and sale merchandise—not just one lone sale rack at the back of the store. A cult favorite for shoppers in the know is the annual Nordstrom Anniversary Sale for men and women in July. The best sales are always the ones where *new* merchandise is discounted.

Many people love to shop sale racks and almost never buy anything full price. Human nature, savvy retailers, and a desire for something new keep us returning to the racks each season. But inevitably, sale racks are full of castaways and end-of-season markdowns. This means we walk away with great bargains (or leftovers) that can't be worn until the weather changes. This can be beneficial for fashion-forward planners searching for next year's treasures or end-of-season prowlers collecting goods, but not everyone!

Tasha is one of many women caught in the web of end-of-season sale shopping. When I first met her, we started shopping her closet to get a sense of her style. Although she shopped all the time, she somehow felt she had nothing to wear. We analyzed her love of couponing and set up an e-mail account to help keep her up to date on available discounts. We discussed her style needs and her budget, and discovered that the thrill she received from finding a great bargain was interfering with the development of her professional image. The most important lesson Tasha learned though the process was how to shop stores she could afford, instead of always hitting stores where she could shop only the sale rack.

Like Tasha, many shoppers feel a lot of pressure when shopping sale racks for basics (something sales are not known for). We often make compromises by buying pieces in the wrong size or color based on price. It was eye-opening for Tasha to go into a store she never would have considered, but one where she could actually afford everything without blinking an eye. Finally, she could invest time, energy, and money in work basics and supplement with pop pieces marked down at the outlets.

The smartest strategy for shopping sales is to keep your list by your side so you are not distracted by prices. Save sales for when you have a little extra to spend in your budget or are searching for a special piece to supplement well-coordinated basics hanging in your closet. Get to know salespeople or personal shoppers at stores for insider access and early notice.

Online Shopping

Online shopping is a popular, time-saving way to shop. Many online outlets carry much larger inventories than their brick-and-mortar counterparts, and weekday lunchtime flash sales can be addicting. If you are not an experienced online shopper, limit your use to replenishment items, accessories, or pieces you tried on in-store that weren't available in your size or desired color. Fashion-seeking hounds may want to hunt down last season's designer shoes and bags that are no longer available in stores but are still fabulous.

If you have an eye for shopping styles without trying them on, be sure to understand return policies before making a final purchase. Many websites will let you know if an item is available locally; this is a great way to try on pieces before making an online purchase. Online shopping can be so easy, especially with one-click speed shopping, that it's not a good idea to do it when you're bored or after a couple glasses of wine. Shopping is like snacking—don't go to the grocery store hungry and don't shop when you're in need of last-minute items. In both cases, you may come home with stuff you don't really like or need.

Any time you shop online, you should search for coupons and free shipping codes. Look on the website you are shopping for a code and check sites like RetailMeNot.com and Savings.com (among many others) that specialize in sharing coupon codes for free. Set up price alerts, be sure to shop Cyber Monday (right after Thanksgiving weekend) for major discounts, and bring proof of online prices to stores for unexpected price matches.

Parting Thoughts

Sometimes, just taking a few moments to breathe in a little fashion is all you need to realize how long it's been since you went shopping. My clients often report that the most relaxing part of their day was the fifteen minutes before our shopping appointment, when they took time to just sit, enjoy a cup of coffee, catch up on personal e-mail, and browse a magazine or store catalogue. This can be a constructive time, because it opens your mind to style creativity.

SHOPPING DESTINATIONS FOR
WORK STAPLES ACROSS THE COUNTRY

The selection of these stores is based on layout and visual appeal, size availability, quality of merchandise, and ease of checkout. Department stores make it easy to shop head-to-toe looks from business formal to business casual. Chain stores are smaller and less intimidating, and offer well-organized career apparel in an easy-to-shop atmosphere.

Shopping is *my* sport of choice, and these destinations make it easy for me to shop for work-wear essentials. There are also many independent boutiques and custom clothing stores all over the country, so be sure to familiarize yourself with your local options.

Department Stores

High budget

- Barneys, barneys.com
- Bergdorf Goodman, bergdorfgoodman.com
- Neiman Marcus, neimanmarcus.com
- Saks Fifth Avenue, saksfifthavenue.com

Moderate

- Bloomingdales, bloomingdales.com
- Dillard's, dillards.com
- Lord & Taylor, lordandtaylor.com
- Macy's, macys.com
- Nordstrom, nordstrom.com

Budget conscious

- Belk, belk.com
- Bon-Ton, bonton.com

(Continued)

- JCPenney, jcpenney.com
- Kohl's, kohls.com
- Sears, sears.com
- Target, target.com
- Von Maur, vonmaur.com
- Walmart, walmart.com

Chain Stores

Men and women

- Banana Republic, bananarepublic.com
- Benetton, benetton.com
- BOSS Hugo Boss, hugoboss.com
- Brooks Brothers, brooksbrothers.com
- Club Monaco, clubmonaco.com
- Elie Tahari, elietahari.com
- Express, express.com
- Forever 21, forever21.com
- H&M, hm.com/us
- J. Crew, jcrew.com
- Reiss, reiss.com/us
- Theory, theory.com
- The Limited, thelimited.com
- Thomas Pink, us.thomaspink.com
- Topshop, us.topshop.com
- Zara, zara.com

Women only

- Ann Taylor, anntaylor.com
- Ann Taylor LOFT, loft.com
- BCBGMAXAZRIA, bcbg.com
- Karen Millen, us.karenmillen.com
- New York and Company, nyandcompany.com
- Talbots, talbots.com
- White House | Black Market, whitehouseblackmarket.com

Men only

- Bonobos, bonobos.com
- Ermenegildo Zegna Boutique, zegna.com/us/
- Jack Spade, jackspade.com
- Jos. A. Bank, josbank.com
- Men's Wearhouse, menswearhouse.com
- Suit Supply, us.suitsupply.com

Online only shopping destinations abound. Find the top five to seven sites that you can manageably surf and bookmark them. The following pair nicely with the bricks and mortar recommendations listed and offer unique merchandise, various price points, and ease of shipping and return policies.

Online only

- Zappos.com and Couture.Zappos.com (Men and Women)
- Bluefly.com (Men and Women)
- Asos.com (Men and Women)
- NET-A-PORTER.com and TheOutnet.com (Women)
- Mrporter.com (Men)

10

LIFE IN THE SPOTLIGHT

We all know celebrities in the entertainment world work with stylists. And rightly so, because even being photographed on a Saturday afternoon running errands is part of their "branding." Each time they land in the pages of a magazine for their great style, another endorsement opportunity may present itself. Working with a stylist isn't considered a luxury for them; it can help them grow their careers.

The same is true for other, less-talked-about groups in the limelight: politicians, CEOs, media professionals, athletes, authors, and motivational speakers. These professionals' images can affect their votes, sales, ratings, public performances, and bookings. Wearing the right color, making sure they're comfortable enough to shake hundreds of hands, identifying the clothing that is strong both on-camera and off, and dressing for sitting on a couch or standing behind a podium can help put public figures and professionals ahead of the competition.

The moment something goes wrong—or viral—VIPs have a team of agents standing by to help manage a crisis. But it's not just celebrities—we all need to be aware and intelligent about protecting our own status and image, online and off.

Online Profile Styling for Everyone

In today's digital world, life is a public stage, and employees are on display both during the workday and online. Recruiters and employers consistently turn to the Internet when researching potential applicants; therefore, it is crucial to manage your online visual résumé. Consider your profiles, especially those on LinkedIn, Twitter, Facebook, and Google+, public forums that colleagues and clients might investigate.

Everyone is a celebrity online! Social media immortalizes not just the individual but your outfit as well. If you dress up your smile with a touch of makeup, your headshot on LinkedIn might just get you an interview. Or, belt a dress and watch five pounds disappear in your company's group portrait. An awkward and dated photo will make you look (and feel) old. Just as in real life, online image matters in business. Don't be overlooked by potential clients—keep your online presence current and stylish. Practice flattering poses and invest in capturing an effective headshot or at least a decent portrait.

Be proactive in managing your image by posting only those photos that communicate an organized, professional image, and keep a sharp eye out for pictures of you posted or tagged by others. Expect that those pictures will be seen by colleagues at the office, and become your own public relations expert.

Each social network focuses on a different demographic, and ones that skew more professional, like LinkedIn, should have an accompanying professional photograph. If you are looking for a job and expect to be taken seriously, cropping yourself out of a party picture does not cut it.

In pictures on Facebook, and elsewhere online (Google yourself to check in), make sure your outfits are varied. Women can take cues from media and political style leaders like First Lady Michelle Obama and Kate Middleton, the Duchess of Cambridge, by changing accessories to freshen a look. You can be perceived as economically savvy when you rewear and restyle ensembles; just avoid wearing the exact same one in every picture. Develop a signature style and always try to look like *you*.

You may already have your dream job, but when you're ready for a photo shoot, take it seriously. Think about how you want your headshot used and what the industry dress code dictates. This picture will be your primary online representation for clients (both current and prospective), out-of-town colleagues, the media, employers, or any organizations you may choose to join. Ladies, to look like a VIP, plan to get your hair and makeup done on the day of your photo shoot. You don't have to go overboard: schedule a seasonal haircut or just a blowout appointment. Visit your favorite makeup artist at her counter, or have someone come to your home. Remember, you want to look authentic and natural. Your hair and makeup help communicate that message. At the very least, do your best to tame flyaways and frizzy hair, and add a touch of lipstick for an extra pop.

As for what to wear, bold solid colors look best for headshots. Framing matters most—remember that your viewer will most likely see you only from the chest up. Your hair and face should garner the most attention, followed by your neckline, accessories, and, finally, your clothes. If you work in a business-formal environment, try not to be pictured going sleeveless, though that might pass muster in other industries that do not enforce a business-formal dress code.

A sheath dress with a bold necklace and stud earrings, or a power third piece with a necklace or stylish earrings, can exude strength. Try on various accessories and bring two to three wardrobe changes. Look in the bathroom mirror (this is the only time I advise looking at yourself strictly from the waist up), and keep playing with your look until you feel confident.

Gentlemen, plan to get your hair cut three to five days before your scheduled headshot, and arrive freshly groomed. If you don't think you will update your picture regularly, opt to dress up rather than down for continued longevity, and bring along a couple of wardrobe changes. Depending on your dress code and need for versatility, take pictures wearing your jacket and tie, just your shirt and tie, and then a dress shirt for a more casual look. If you prefer to wear solids, white shirts stand out well against the traditional gray background of a headshot photo, and bold ties are an easy match. For the fashion-inclined, mix patterns and stripes, but do your best to avoid overloading the eyes with busy patterns.

If you wear glasses intermittently, try pictures featuring them both on and off. If you are self-employed and taking portraits for your website in addition to a simple headshot, definitely indulge in outfit changes and dressing up as well as down to reach different target markets. Keep in mind that as you move from headshot to portrait, the camera angle widens to include more of your ensemble. Make sure your clothing fits well—avoid anything baggy. Women should rock belts, bold necklaces, and heels to help flatter their shapes; men should use color to draw attention. For a well-rounded photo shoot, wear clothing that works for seated as well as action shots.

To lead a successful life in the virtual limelight, keep your online visual identity consistent. Use the same pictures across different professional networks and update them every few years. Follow these tips and, like any VIP, you will become instantly recognizable when you walk into the room.

Crafting Your Public Persona

I love packing clients for business trips. It is the only time I can (mostly) control everything they wear! Shopping your suitcase can be liberating because your options are far fewer than in your closet. When I pack for clients I coordinate outfits, take pictures, and show them exactly how to mix and match.

Of course, though I may shop with and for clients, I certainly can't force them to wear the exact combinations I've selected. I am more of a style tutor than an enforcer. Not all of my clients are aiming for a spot on the best-dressed list; they just want to be taken seriously. Clothes are a big part of their image, though they are far from the only factor at play.

Victoria was an elected official who hired me to help with her reelection campaign. She was facing a tough election season, and refreshing her overall image was a necessity. She had inherited her seat and felt she had a lot to prove in order to keep it. We worked on simple body-language tactics, focusing on her posture. As a mom of three, she was used to slumping over in what I call "caretaker mode." I taught her to suck in her midsection (Kegel exercises are a good addition to this trick), roll out her ribs, and push her shoulders back. Magically, she grew two inches.

Good posture and a friendly smile are inexpensive yet effective tools in your arsenal. Have someone take a short video of you sitting at your desk or leading a meeting in a conference room, and take note of the placement of your shoulders and midsection. Are your shoulders rounded instead of straight? Is your belly sticking out instead of flexed? Many of us are so relaxed in our movements that we don't pay much attention to what our bodies are saying. It's certainly not an easy habit to correct, but it is one that will be easily noted by your audience. Imagine a president or general who led with slumped shoulders or an insecure gait—she wouldn't be very effective at rallying the troops! The best way to know if you have good posture and presence is to feel it. If you're aware of sitting or standing tall and flexing your muscles, then you're on the right track.

Victoria and I traveled from television appearances to parades as I watched her in action. This everyday woman needed to have a commanding presence while capturing the hearts of many. She had to remain accessible yet be distinctive. I shopped for the perfect pieces and worked with designers and tailors to create unique touches suitable for a public official. She needed pockets in her clothing but less bulkiness on her hips. Wrinkle-free and easy-to-pack clothing choices were essential (but so was bringing along a good steamer). Breathable, moveable clothes were important in this situation as well. In "Pollywood," as opposed to Hollywood, folks easily live in their clothes for twelve hours before a wardrobe change. I style outfits and accessories that can be layered throughout the day and paired with comfortable and stylish shoes.

Victoria's challenge was connecting with her audience. An average-size woman, a 12, who favored wearing traffic-stopping, busy patterns instead of the bold and slimming colors of leadership, she was missing an opportunity to capture everyone's attention with her message. By dressing in a sleek, monochromatic color palette, you can encourage your audience to remain focused on you and your message. For example, the most successful news anchors wear one solid color on television instead of patterns. The same is true when speaking in front of large groups—you should strive to be the exclamation mark, not a run-on sentence.

Campaigning in the spring, Victoria found that her favorite outfits on the trail were sheath dresses in bright colors like fuchsia, sherbet orange, sky blue, and kelly green, with matching or coordinating dress-length jackets or shorter, belted cardigans. Victoria's signature style began to emerge and not only captured everyone's attention but also mirrored her political style: bold, modern, and concise.

Color can inspire emotion and keep the public engaged. Joey was a motivational speaker who wrote incredible books and had a captivating voice. Yet on camera or onstage, he lacked presence. He favored dowdy earth tones, and his appearance was never as neatly packaged as his message. The same was true for Lucia, a health-care expert who often appeared on news broadcasts. When I first started working with Lucia, we would meet in the green room at any of the cable news studios where she frequently appeared, ready to go on air wearing unflatteringly loose, drab, and unstylish clothing. Sometimes the best I could do was pop her collar and tighten the belt on her dress!

I used the same tutorials to give both Lucia and Joey a color education. I don't use science to determine your best colors (or fits) as much as try to make you aware of what can work with your coloring, shape, and environment. For example, wearing blue sets a peaceful tone, calms people, and encourages them to trust you—it's a great color when you're speaking about something controversial. Red, a fire color, is good for bold topics and projecting confidence. Lessons on color as well as fit are crucial to those in the public eye. The camera and stage add weight and wash you out so make sure your clothing works with you and not against you.

Limelight Etiquette

If you don't have an entourage around to help you in a fashion emergency, it can be hard to know just what to do. In fact, the etiquette of public appearances can be confusing for many. One of the most common issues in the summer months is helping men stay stylish in the heat. It is surprising how many wipe sweat from their face with their bare hands. I see many men do this while on live television! This habit is not only unsightly and unhygienic, it also communicates deception and nervousness. It can be easily remedied with a handkerchief tucked into the back pocket. I often give clients monogrammed hankies as gifts to encourage the right habit.

Have you ever leaned over to tell someone in your dinner party she has smeared lipstick or something stuck in her teeth? If you are a VIP, chances are you have an aide or personal assistant nearby whose job description includes such personal matters. Everyone else must learn the tricks of managing his own image! If you tend to get food in your teeth, carry a small mirror and discreetly sneak a quick look to check.

Style Alert: *If your crowd embraces technology during mealtimes and phones are on the table, pretend to check e-mail and switch your device to camera mode. Go all "007" and change the direction of the camera to face you so it acts like a mirror—voilà!*

Professions in the public eye, even those with a lower profile, need to know all the tricks. Those with the best eyeglasses (that avoid adding wrinkles or glare), hairstyles (low fuss), makeup (natural and flawless), and signature style are always among the most successful. They do not take a step into the television studio or onto the public stage until they've checked and rechecked their appearances. Even a hair out of place can be distracting when all eyes will be on them for an extended period.

But it's not just VIPs who should learn how to own a room and feel confident about their image. Interns need to know the beauty of a firm handshake and elected officials the secret of a good half hug. It is a practical skill to know how to properly greet people and refrain from fidgeting. Take a cue from on-air journalists and celebrities. They rarely touch their faces or hair while on stage or working. Whether you are a mom or dad, single or married, and whether you work in media, technology, science, government, finance, law, or any other profession, you want to be the best at what you do.

Entitlement Dressing

"Entitlement dressing" is a term I've coined for successful people who *don't* dress to impress anyone. They show up at meetings deliberately dressed more casually than everyone else and live by their own interesting interpretation of dress codes. These might be consultants or partners wearing causal attire when others are in suits, or members of Congress and elected local officials wearing jeans, hats, or cowboy boots when no one else is (or should be). These individuals are neither stylish nor frumpy; they confidently use their seniority to prove they don't have to conform.

Think carefully about how you want to be perceived as a leader. Most CEOs would not dream of dressing down like this unless it matched their corporate culture. While a casual or careless style might work personally for a confident individual, it sets a poor example for anyone working on his team. It is always effective to create a signature style, but don't adopt one that is isolating unless you are a style star lighting up the room. When you dress like an entitled individual, you are essentially saying the rules don't apply to you.

Parting Thoughts

You now know that style matters. Your image doesn't need to change overnight—take it one step at a time. Look in the mirror and ask yourself truly how many elements of your image are within your control. You can't always manipulate your physical look or even your budget, but the style of clothes you buy, the type of makeup you wear, the way you style your hair, you—and only you—are responsible for this.

Open your closet and look inside. Clean it out. Identify any gaps in your wardrobe and create your shopping list. Schedule time for yourself and make a commitment to owning your image.

If you find yourself at a loss or confused when creating your professional persona, find a muse. Identify a style mentor, friend, relative, fashion blogger, or character on television who you think looks professional (like Alicia Florrick and Diane Lockhart on *The Good Wife,* Neal Caffrey on *White Collar,* or Don Draper on *Mad Men*). Bookmark websites, tear out style ensembles from catalogues or magazines, or grab your *Style Bible* and start studying. Continue to explore your ideal image until you feel confident enough to snag the job—or anything else—you want!

LAUREN'S STYLIST REPAIR KIT

I like to keep these essentials on hand for any last-minute fashion emergencies in the C-suite (or closet):

- Hollywood deodorant-removing sponge: Use this sponge to remove a spot of deodorant or makeup from your clothes.
- Double-stick tape: Take care of gaping in your blouse, straps that go astray, or hems that come apart at the last minute.
- Small sewing kit: Fix a button, small tear, or hole on the go. Be sure to have a handy stack of safety pins for last-minute fixes in a pinch.
- Clever Clasp necklace extender: This magnetic wonder immediately extends the length of any necklace and comes in both silver and gold tones of varying lengths.
- Shoe insoles and blister relief: A long day walking the office runway can leave you with sore feet. Don't say no to drinks after work just because your feet are tired.
- On-the-go galoshes: Protect your shoes in case you have a last-minute client meeting on a rainy day. Shuellas and Swims fold up in your bag for portable style.

- Shoe brush and protective rejuvenating spray for suede accessories and a Kiwi shoe-shine sponge for leather shoes: be ready to spiff up your walking shoes before a big entrance.
- Tide To-Go stain-remover pen: Catch a stray stain before it makes a permanent home.
- Lint roller: Remove pet hair or unwanted sweater fuzz.
- Static Guard: Use this dual-purpose spray to control frizz and flyaways for your hair as well as static cling in your clothes.
- Hair mascara wand: Look younger in minutes and cover grays if you haven't had time to run to the salon.
- Hand moisturizer: Many people talk with their hands. Keep yours looking fresh and moisturized.
- Nail file, Sally Hansen nail-white pencil, and clear nail polish: Give yourself an instant, easy manicure.
- Aquaphor: Use this ointment for instant lip repair and shine, and to treat minor cuts.
- Energy bar: Be prepared in case you miss a meal (or two).
- Breath mints: You've achieved the perfect look. Don't lose a client at "hello."

ACKNOWLEDGMENTS

First and foremost, thank you to all the men and women who have invited me into their closets and followed me into the fitting room. Writing a book about what to wear to work would not be possible without the many companies who graciously welcomed me onto their office runways. I feel a special sense of gratitude toward the retail community for always providing a haven for retail therapy and maintaining long holiday shopping hours every year (they are simply the best!).

Thank you to my agent Ron Goldfarb and his associate Gerrie Sturman, my publishers Erika Heilman and Jill Friedlander at Bibliomotion, and to publicists Kaila Nickel and Rusty Shelton. A special thanks to creative magicians and visionaries: *Style Bible* illustrator Kristina Hultkrantz, graphic and web designer Johanna Guevara-Smiley, photographer Rashmi Pappu, and filmmakers Othello Banachi and Justin French.

I am so profoundly grateful to the Styleauteur team: social media experts Stephanie Klejst and Sonia Gaillis-Delepine; my talented glam squad: Nuri Yurt, Yaneek Proctor, and Blanton Brown; and, my crack financial team: Dannette Wolf and George Woglom. Thank you to editors extraordinaire Jill Schoenhaut, Caroline Schweiter, Alison Carroll, and Andrea Tecce for their contributions and knowledge to helping make *Style Bible* a success.

I want to thank my friends in the media who were early supporters of my message and continue to put me in front of a camera or interview me for a story. I am grateful to the teams at CNN en Español and Entertainment Tonight for continuing to use me as a resource on air. A special thank you to Ryan Grim at The Huffington Post for helping me develop my Fashion Whip column, and to the Let's Talk Live family in Washington, DC: fabulous and talented producers Alison Kenworthy, AnnaMaria Di Pietro, and Laura Chavez and hosts Natasha Barrett and Melanie Hastings who have been endlessly supportive and have featured me on their show once-a-month since 2009.

I am very appreciative of my work experiences as they have taught me many valuable lessons. Internships are truly a blessing and I am thankful to *Elle* magazine, MTV Networks, and the United States House of Representatives. Thank you to Faith Popcorn's BrainReserve for training in trend-forecasting that is equivalent to a Master's degree; and to Nordstrom and Saks Fifth Avenue for the ultimate lessons in customer service.

Thank you to my lifelong friends for your inspirational pep talks, moral support, and helping me keep my sanity while writing: Silvana Garcia, Mindy Wright, Debbie Jones, Christy Boullon, Elizan Garcia, Samantha Durso, Naima Jefferson, Irene Jones, and Sarah Boyd. A special thank you to Danielle Loevin for your bravery in allowing me to share our story, and to Ella McManus for encouraging my vision since the day we met. I am also grateful to all of my Facebook, Twitter, and LinkedIn publicists: you help spread the word about *Style Bible* every day!

My crazy book-writing schedule (and career) would not be as successful without the loving support of my amazing family. Thank you to my parents for working hard to provide me with every opportunity and helping to shape my love of heels and 'the look for less' from an early age. Dad, your detailed feedback and your endless energy and enthusiasm every step of the way is contagious. Mami, you taught me to love fashion and style and to help others without judgment or reservation. To my stylish in-laws, Steve and Marlene Gerbsman: Your unwavering support since I met you both at Colby dressed in matching North Face down vests is appreciated more than you will ever know. Steve, thank you for allowing me to continue to style you, and Marlene, you are a mentor both as a best-dressed woman and mom.

It takes a village to raise a family and mine would not be complete without the help of Susana Muñoz: gracias por cuidar nuestra familia como si fuera la tuya. My son, Judah: I am so happy you share my love of style and our daily dance breaks to practice Gangnam Style moves was truly a highlight throughout my long days of writing. Lastly, a most profound and heartfelt *gracias* to my loving Guapo, Jason. Eighteen years together is not enough. You are my compass. There are not enough words in the dictionary to say thank you.

INDEX

ABOUT THE AUTHOR

Lauren A. Rothman, founder of Styleauteur (www.styleauteur.com), is a fashion, style, and trend expert. She is one of the nation's most sought after stylists and helps shape dress codes at many Fortune 500 companies. She is responsible for famous looks along the campaign trail, as well as subtle styles that have made their way into the halls of the Supreme Court and the front rows of the White House Correspondents' dinner.

Lauren is passionate about working with our servicemen and women returning from overseas deployments and has also counseled four star generals at the Pentagon regarding professional civilian dress. Her mantra underscores that dressing is about much more than the clothes—it is about who you truly are and the image you want to project. Lauren maintains an image therapy practice working with individual and corporate clients to help increase their style quotient.

A trend spotter and fashion maven, Lauren has her finger on the pulse of fashion—from shopping closets across the country to discussing executive presence, political style and First Family fashions on Entertainment Tonight, CNN, E! News, The Insider, AP News, Reuters, and ABC News. Greatly sought after as a public speaker and style commentator from Silicon Valley to New York City, her tips on wardrobe management and creating a versatile, fashion-forward closet have been featured in *Glamour, Real Simple, People StyleWatch, The Washington Post, The New York Post*, Politico, and Oprah.com as well as on NPR and SiriusXM radio. Lauren also discusses executive presence and political style in her column, "Fashion Whip," in The Huffington Post.

Lauren studied at the University of Salamanca in Spain and graduated cum laude from Colby College in Waterville, Maine with a major in English literature. She got her start as an intern at *Elle* magazine and her wide-ranging experience includes positions as a cool hunter at Faith Popcorn's BrainReserve and a wardrobe consultant at Nordstrom and Saks Fifth Avenue. Lauren lives with her husband, son, and pink-toenail- polished Dogue de Bordeaux in McLean, Virginia.